Birds Eye War Time
Leicestershire
1939 - 1945

© Wright Process Engravings Co. Ltd.

This photograph shows a tree bedecked by a girder from one of the three large houses which were completely destroyed by a 'Landmine' which fell on the corner of Newstead Street and Knighton Road, on the night of November 19th 1940, with eight fatalities. This tree survives to this day and small pieces of metal can still be seen embedded in the top of the stump.

The above is represented by just a small red star on the City Map (pages 10 & 11)

Acknowledgments & Sources

I would like to thank the many people who have contacted me since the publication of my first book *Birds Eye Wartime Leicester*, also readers of the Leicester Mercury and the Hinckley Times for valuable clues to solve the many complex incidents presented in this work, which would not have been complete without their help. I regret that to list all would take many pages, so much was the interest - So please accept my thanks to you all on this page.

Intelligence Reports and Photographs

Bundersarchiv, Germany.
Public Record Office, Kew, London.
Leicestershire Museums Arts & Record Service.
Beaumanor Hall, Loughborough, Leicestershire.

English Heritage (R.C.H.M.E.), Swindon.
National Archives, Maryland, U.S.A.
Loughborough Library, Leicestershire.
Wright Process Engravings Co. Ltd., Leicester.

I would also like to thank my son Clive, for without his interest and expertise in producing the artwork and maps, this book would never have been published.

Published by T.C.C. Publications
6 The Woodlands, Wigston
Leicestershire LE18 3QE, UK.
(http://www.wartimeleicestershire.com)

Copyright © Terence C. Cartwright, 2002

Cartography & Illustrations by Quirky Media

ISBN 0-9534497-1-8

First published 2002

2 4 6 8 10 9 7 5 3 1

Printed in Great Britain at the De Montfort Press by Raithby, Lawrence & Co Ltd.
18 Slater Street, Frog Island,
Leicester, LE3 5AY, UK.

Photographs: R.A.F., by kind permission M.O.D.
English Heritage, by kind permission.
Maps and Boundaries as 1930's OS Maps. H.M.S.O.

Cover photograph
See Leicestershire Civil Defence plotting map *page 17*.

FOREWORD

Over the years researching for material for my booklet 'Birds Eye Wartime Leicester' I often wondered if I could cover the whole county, but lack of official documents left me with the task of contacting eye witnesses and the use of newspaper reports (which were very limited due to censorship). Having already collated some very interesting aerial photographs, but wanting to give as complete a picture possible, I decided to abandon the idea and concentrate on the city. However, directly after the publication of 'Birds Eye Wartime Leicester', many readers wrote with new information; one in particular advised of the existence of the actual bomb plotting map as used by the Leicestershire A.R.P. (now stored at Beaumanor Hall) and this combined with the acquisition of the excellent 'Civil Defence in Leicestershire 1935-1945' book by James McDougall, provided a good foundation for me to produce this book. Like my last book, the main purpose is to present this as a "public awareness exercise". Many pages could have been written on any one incident or area (particularly the airfields) so I must ask enthusiasts to forgive me for not going into any great depth and refer to the bibliography for sources.

I have also taken this opportunity to include an updated bomb map of the city. Not many changes, but it does now show the locations of the missing UXB's and a handful of bombs which I had missed in my last book.

The information contained within is my own interpretation of events after sifting through many official, eye witness and newspaper reports. You would be amazed at the differing accounts I have had concerning some incidents! Failing memories and "Chinese whispers" combined with inaccurate reports have been a nightmare to process. Errors and omissions will no doubt be found and I therefore welcome any criticism or correction on any aspect in order to ensure my database is as complete and correct as possible.

On looking at the pattern of the bomb fall it would appear that anyone living near railway stations, goods yards and junctions were at most risk, followed by those living near searchlight batteries. The first being a primary opportunistic target for forced jettisons and secondly I understand that aircraft "coned" by searchlights would drop their bombs on the site (if possible) or jettison in order to take evasive action.

As the war progressed, the threat of being "dispatched" by a bomb was replaced by a similar threat from falling aircraft! They were falling like autumn leaves but due to severe censorship, very few people knew and even now know of these crashes unless an aircraft fell in their back garden!

Younger readers who have heard the comment "I remember when this was all fields and allotments" will be able to share this memory through the following pages.

I dedicate this book not only to the generation who experienced these events but also the young and future generations who, I hope, will realise that knowledge of the past provides wisdom to create a better future!

Terence C. Cartwright
December 2001

Contents

GB
Geheim

Leicester

DT/TM-3/Great Britain, Leicester/Neg No. 72
N52 W1

Karte 1:100 000/163 Sch
Blatt   Blatt
17   63

Kriegsschäden
468 R 68

Länge westw. Greenw: 1° 7′30 Breite 52° 37′ 0
Mißweisung 11°35′ Mitte 1935

Nachtrag:
8.6.39.

500   500   1000
                                          m
Maßstab etwa 16 000   etwa 160 m

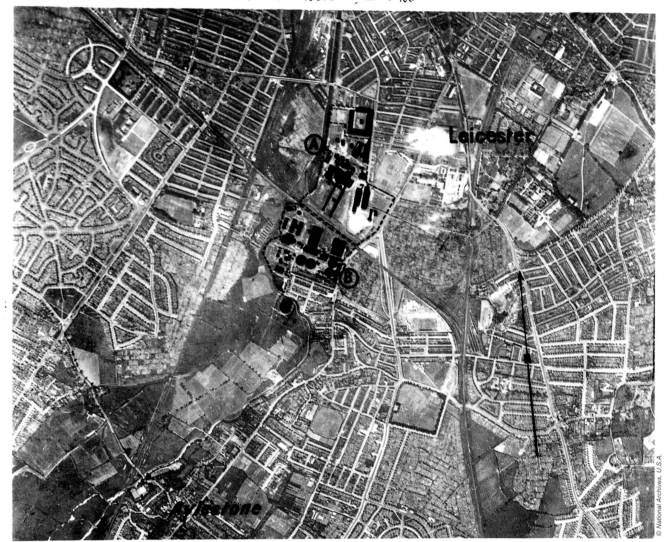

© National Archives, U.S.A.

(A)   GB 509   G r o ß k r a f t w e r k

1)	1 Kesselhaus	etwa	5 400 qm
2)	1 Maschinenhaus	etwa	4 700 qm
3)	6 Kühltürme je etwa 30m Ø		
4)	1 Kohlenförderanlage	etwa	500 qm
5)	1 Freiluft Umspannwerk	etwa	3 600 qm
6)	3 Transformatorenhäuser	etwa	1 500 qm
7)	4 Verwaltungs-u. Werkgebäude	etwa	11 000 qm
8)	1 Kraftwagenhaus	etwa	1 000 qm
9)	1 Bürogeb., Zugehörigk. z. Kw. fraglich		
	bebaute Fläche	etwa	27 700 qm

Ausdehnung insgesamt   etwa 225 000 qm
Gleisanschluß vorhanden

(B)   GB   G a s w e r k

1)	2 Gasgewinnungsöfen	etwa	14 000 qm
2)	Gasreinigungs- und Destillationsanlage	etwa	15 000 qm
3)	2 Tanks für Destillations-Zwischenprodukte 16 u. 25m Ø		
4)	5 Gasometer, 1Stck. 64m, u. 4 Stck. je 56m Ø		
5)	15 Nebengebäude	etwa	4 000 qm
	bebaute Fläche	etwa	33 000 qm

Ausdehnung insgesamt   etwa 150 000 qm

Gleisanschluß vorhanden

AYLESTONE: Luftwaffe photograph taken June 8th 1939 highlighting the Power Station and Gas Works.

Note that Filbert Street Football Ground was, for reasons unknown, included within the target boundary (broken line).

CITY GAS WORKS: Luftwaffe photograph taken December 15th 1940. The City Power Station and Filbert Street.

This aircraft was picked up on RADAR and although fighter planes were "scrambled" from Group 10, all attempts to intercept, failed.

Luftwaffe Target Maps

In 1939, whilst Neville Chamberlain was running around waving pieces of paper proclaiming "peace in our time", Luftwaffe intelligence units were quietly and methodically photographing most of the UK in order to identify and record all strategic/ military installations. Railway stations, goods yards, power stations, gasworks and heavy engineering works were considered primary targets. Waterworks, pumping stations and other engineering works were classed as secondary targets.

Photographs were marked up accordingly and these were highlighted on 1930's ordnance survey maps (Hitler did not ask permission I understand!). Major targets were outlined in red, secondary targets in purple and optional targets were marked with symbols. Hospitals were outlined in red but also marked with a red cross. These maps were issued to bomber crews to study before any attack. Every attack on the UK was planned down to the last detail, crews were each assigned targets/target areas, bombs loads and types of bombs were arranged to suit the intended targets, even times over target were planned. The maps printed on pages 8 & 9 show two of the four which covered the city of Leicester.

FILBERT STREET: Enlargement of the top photograph showing Filbert Street stadium and the Tigers ground. On close scrutiny can be seen the hole in the roof of the stand *(arrowed)* made by the bomb. Other craters in the area appear to have been filled in.

The above photographs taken on December 15th 1940 by a German reconnaissance aircraft for damage assessment, shows the area of the target map photo *(page 2)*. In spite of at least 24 high explosive bombs and many hundreds of incendiaries having fallen on this area German intelligence must have been very disappointed to see very little damage, apart from the craters in the cricket ground and the damage to the city football ground stand *(arrowed)*. However, with the Tigers stand burnt down, bombs on the cricket ground and the damaged stand at Filbert Street, they could claim to have scored a "hat-trick" on Leicester's sporting facilities!

GB

Leicester

DT/TM-3/Great Britain, Leicester/Neg No. 84
N52 W1

17 | 63

468 R 65

Länge (westl.Greenw.) 1° 12′ 20″, Breite 52° 38′ 0″
Mißweisung:-11°32′ (Mitte 1938)

24.5.39

500   0   500   1000

Maßstab etwa 1 : 15 000   (1cm = 150m)

© National Archives, U.S.A.

nach Leicester (Mitte)
5,2 km Luftlinie

900m

700m

Ⓐ GB 10 126 F l u g p l a t z

1) 3 Hallen   etwa   2 500 qm
2) 4 Flughafengebäude etwa   1 500 qm
3) 2 eingelassene Tanks etwa 30m ∅
4) 1 Kompensierscheibe
   _____
   bebaute Fläche   etwa 4 000 qm

Gleisanschluß nicht vorhanden
Erweiterung möglich

BRAUNSTONE FRITH: Luftwaffe photograph taken May 24th 1939. Marked up target is Leicester Municipal Aerodrome.

The following photographs further illustrate how the Luftwaffe had their sights set firmly on all existing airfield's throughout Leicestershire months before Neville Chamberlain declared war on Germany. Leicester Municipal *(above)* originally started out life as a private grass field station during the mid 1930's catering for early commercial flights from Leicester. However, during the outbreak of war, the R.A.F. commissioned this airfield as a satellite for the No.7 Elementary Flying School De Havilland Tiger Moth's, based at Desford. The restricted size of the airfield proved to be a constant cause for concern as the war progressed, and on numerous occasions planes were found crashing through the airfield's boundary hedge. As a result, Braunstone's aerodrome was closed down permanently at the end of the war.

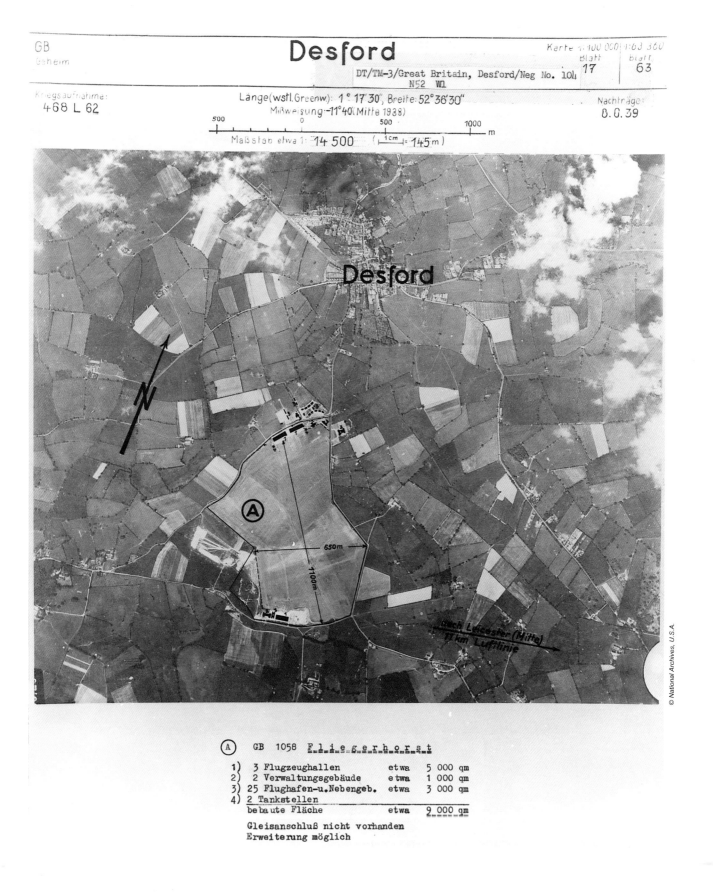

GB
Geheim

Desford

Karte 1:100 000 1:63 360
Blatt 17 | Blatt 63

DT/TM-3/Great Britain, Desford/Neg No. 104
N52 W1

Kriegsaufnahme:
4-68 L 62

Länge(wstl.Greenw): 1°17'30", Breite 52°36'30"
Mißweisung -11°40'(Mitte 1938)

Nachträge:
8.0.39

500   0   500   1000
                              m

Maßstab etwa 1: 14 500   (1cm = 145 m)

© National Archives, U.S.A.

Ⓐ   GB   1058   F l i e g e r h o r s t

1) 3 Flugzeughallen   etwa   5 000 qm
2) 2 Verwaltungsgebäude   etwa   1 000 qm
3) 25 Flughafen-u.Nebengeb. etwa   3 000 qm
4) 2 Tankstellen
   bebaute Fläche   etwa   9 000 qm

Gleisanschluß nicht vorhanden
Erweiterung möglich

DESFORD: Luftwaffe photograph taken June 8th 1939. Marked up target is Desford Aerodrome.

Desford Airfield, approx. 6.5 miles west of Leicester, originally opened as a grass airfield catering for the Elementary and Reserve Flying Training School. By the time the war started, Desford was fully equipped with the De Havilland Tiger Moth, for its continuing role in training pilots. This airfield was also active in aircraft repairs on such aircraft as the Defiant fighter and the assembly of the Supermarine Spitfires.

As the war progressed Desford took on repair work for the American Mitchell B-25 bomber. However, RAF Desford did not pass without its share of aviation incidents. On one such notable occasion, on October 10th 1943, a U.S. B-17 Flying Fortress crash-landed into one of the airfield's southern hangers, injuring two of ten crew on board.

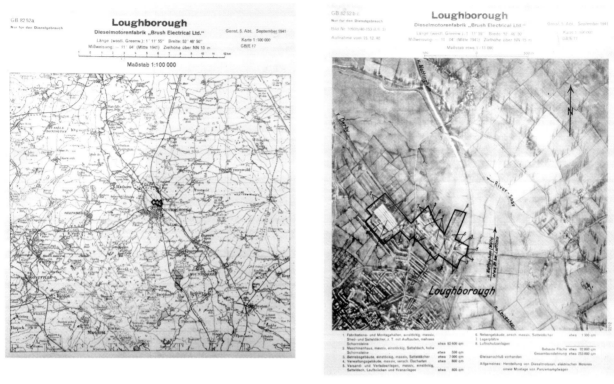

LUFTWAFFE TARGET MAPS: Showing marked up target areas of Brush Works, Loughborough. September 1941.

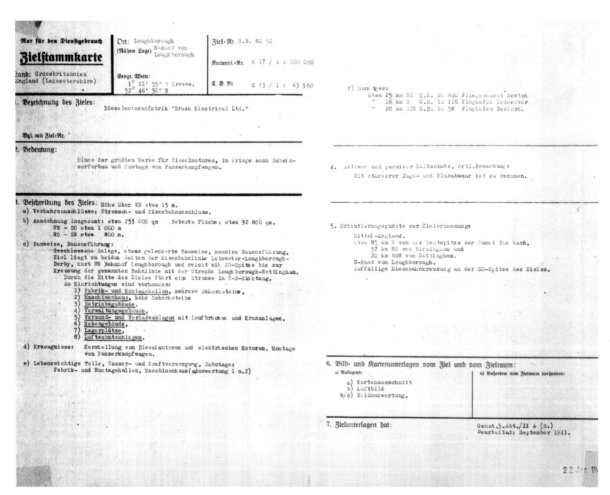

LUFTWAFFE TARGET INFORMATION CARDS: Prepared for use in conjunction with target photographs.

The above three images by courtesy of Loughborough Library, Leicestershire (Brush Collection).

LOUGHBOROUGH: April 4th 1944. Note the airstrip top right and part of the camouflaged Brush Works Ltd. bottom centre.

In spite of all the work preparing target material for the Brush Works it was never subjected to an attack! This could be due to the fact that Luftwaffe intelligence had noted it had it's own air defence site *(see information card, point no.3-C8).*

Loughborough airfield was placed in a state of disuse for the first year of the war but was eventually requisitioned as a repair base, for RAF aircraft during late 1940. Hampden's and de Havilland Dominies were assembled initially, followed by Boston's which were refurbished and converted within hangers off Derby Road, arriving by road in various states of disrepair. By mid 1943 the first of many Boston's started to take off from Loughborough airfield, but not always without incident. One such notable event occurred on February 19th 1944, when a Boston experienced trouble taking off, due to the limited size of the airfield. The Boston stalled and crashed into the Dishley Mill road bridge, on Derby Road.

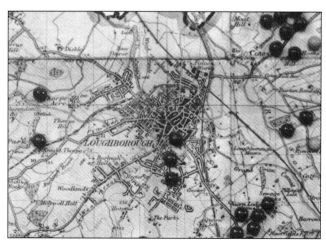

LOUGHBOROUGH: A.R.P. Civil Defence report map, plotting the bomb fall in and around the town.

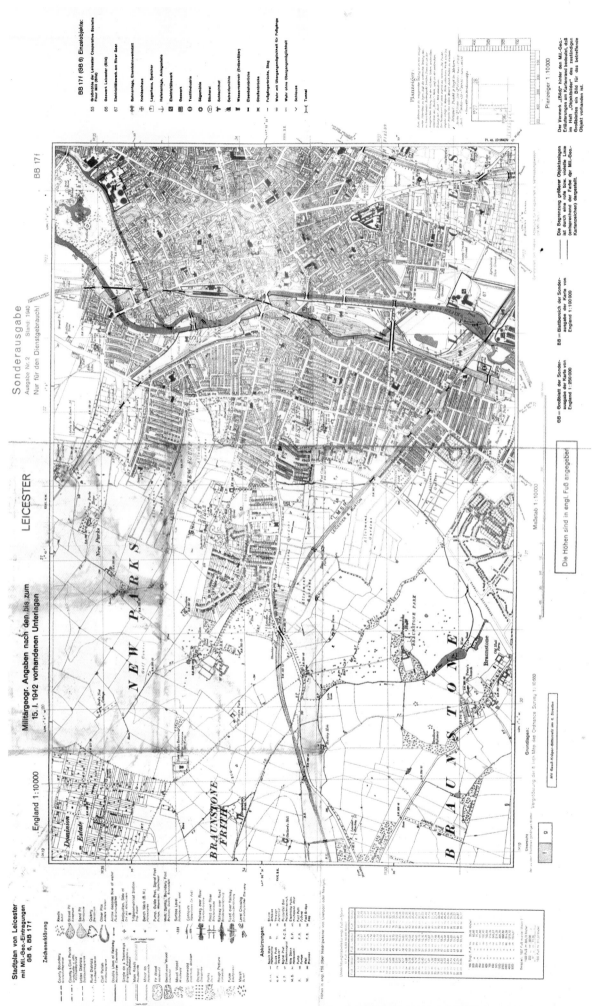

WEST LEICESTER: Luftwaffe Target Map. This map was "captured" by a Bren-Gunner who, during an assault on a German Airfield in Holland, found he was lying on a pile of maps in one of the perimeter buildings (courtesy of Trevor Hickman, Wymondham.)

8

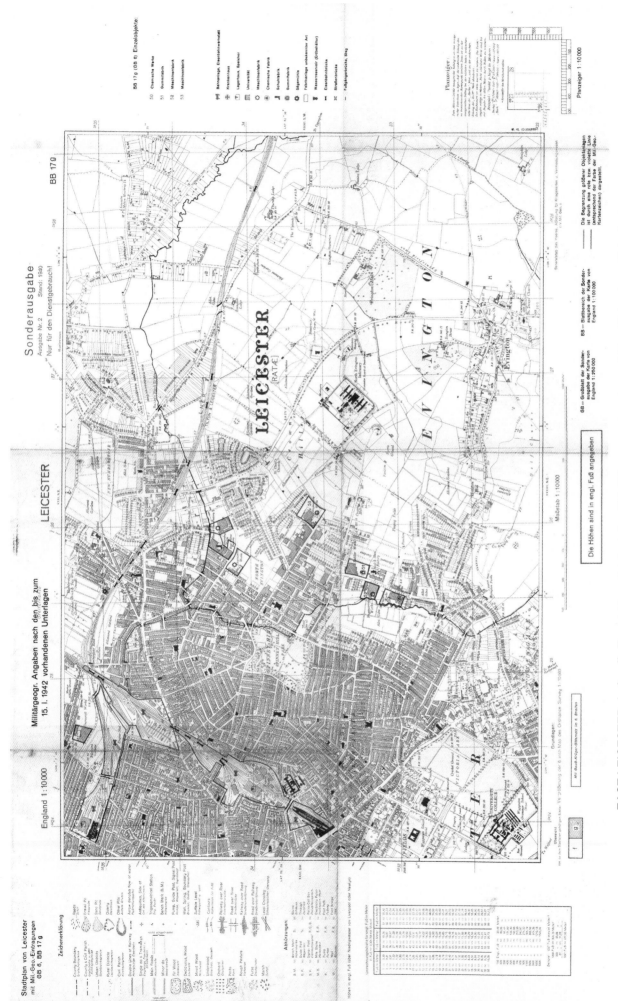

EAST LEICESTER: Luftwaffe Target Map. Original size 20"x30" approx. (courtesy of Alan Richardson, Evington).

9

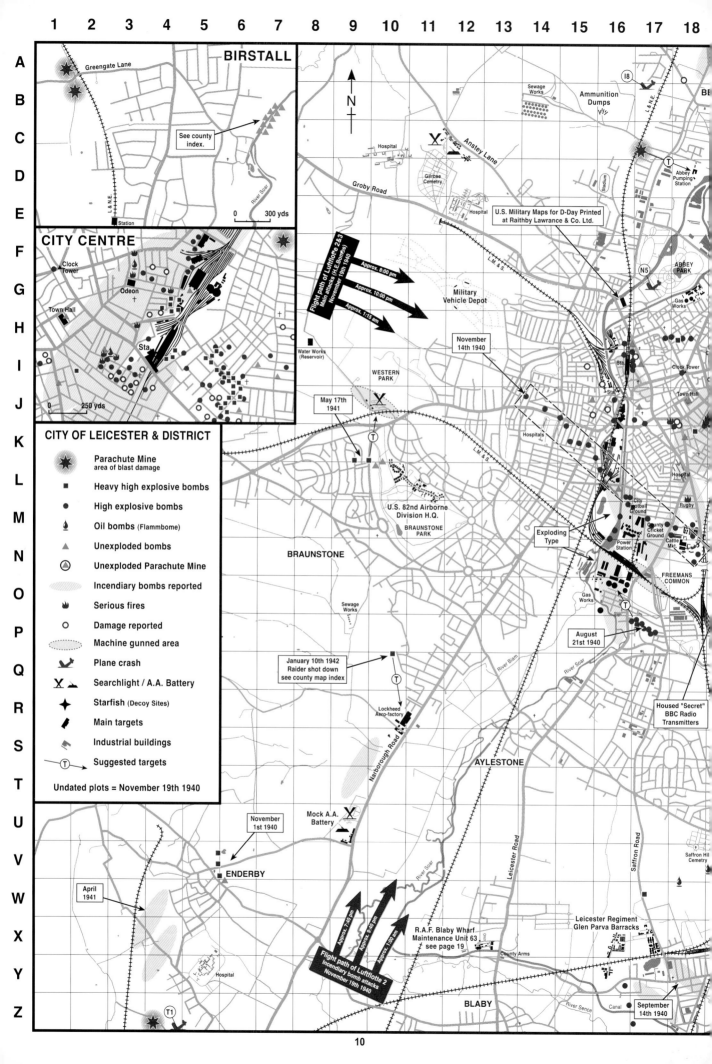

Column numbers: 1 2 3 4 5 6 7 8 9 10 11 12 13 14 15 16 17 18

Row letters: A B C D E F G H I J K L M N O P Q R S T U V W X Y Z

BIRSTALL

Greengate Lane

See county index.

L & N.E.

River Soar

0 300 yds

Station

CITY CENTRE

Clock Tower

Town Hall

Odeon

Sta.

0 250 yds

CITY OF LEICESTER & DISTRICT

- ⚝ **Parachute Mine** area of blast damage
- ■ **Heavy high explosive bombs**
- ● **High explosive bombs**
- ⬥ **Oil bombs** (Flammbome)
- ▲ **Unexploded bombs**
- ⬤ **Unexploded Parachute Mine**
- ▨ **Incendiary bombs reported**
- ♨ **Serious fires**
- ○ **Damage reported**
- ▨ **Machine gunned area**
- ⬇ **Plane crash**
- ✕ **Searchlight / A.A. Battery**
- ✦ **Starfish** (Decoy Sites)
- ◢ **Main targets**
- ◣ **Industrial buildings**
- →(T)→ **Suggested targets**

Undated plots = November 19th 1940

N

Sewage Works

Ammunition Dumps

I8

L & N.E.

BR

Hospital

Anstey Lane

Gilrose Cemetery

Groby Road

Hospital

U.S. Military Maps for D-Day Printed at Raithby Lawrance & Co. Ltd.

Abbey Pumping Station

Stadium

L.M. & S.

N5

ABBEY PARK

Gas Works

Flight path of Luftflotte 2 & 3
Main attacks (H.E.Bombs)
November 19th 1940

Approx. 8:00 pm
Approx. 10:00 pm
Approx. 1:15 am

Military Vehicle Depot

November 14th 1940

Water Works (Reservoir)

WESTERN PARK

Clock Tower

Town Hall

Sta.

Hospitals

May 17th 1941

Exploding Type

Hospital

U.S. 82nd Airborne Division H.Q.

BRAUNSTONE PARK

BRAUNSTONE

Sewage Works

City Football Ground

County Cricket Ground

Cattle Mkt.

Power Station

FREEMANS COMMON

Gas Works

Rugby

August 21st 1940

Housed "Secret" BBC Radio Transmitters

January 10th 1942
Raider shot down
see county map index

Lockheed Aero-factory

River Biam

River Soar

AYLESTONE

Leicester Road

Saffron Road

November 1st 1940

April 1941

Mock A.A. Battery

ENDERBY

River Soar

Saffron Hil Cemetery

Approx. 7:40 pm
Approx. 9:40 pm
Approx. 1:50 am

R.A.F. Blaby Wharf
Maintenance Unit 63
see page 19

County Arms

Leicester Regiment
Glen Parva Barracks

Flight path of Luftflotte 2
incendiary bomb attacks
November 19th 1940

BLABY

River Sence

Canal

September 14th 1940

T1

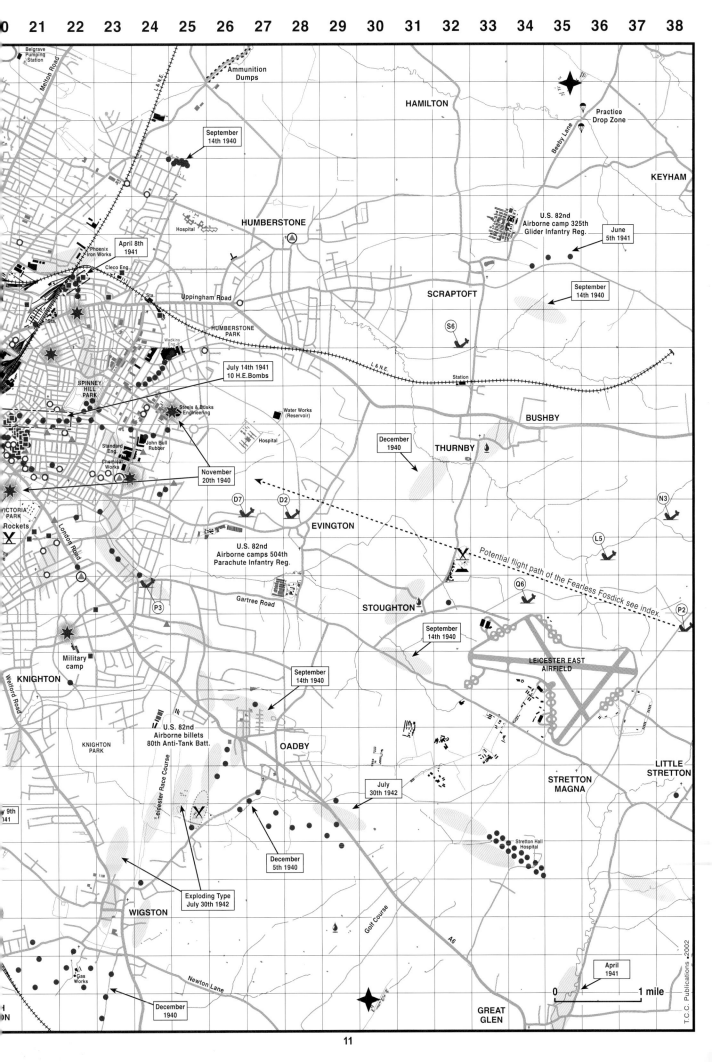

Belgrave Pumping Station

Melton Road

L & N.E.

Ammunition Dumps

September 14th 1940

HAMILTON

Practice Drop Zone

KEYHAM

Beeby Lane

HUMBERSTONE

Hospital

U.S. 82nd Airborne camp 325th Glider Infantry Reg.

June 5th 1941

April 8th 1941

Phoenix Iron Works

Cleco Eng.

Sta.

Uppingham Road

SCRAPTOFT

September 14th 1940

HUMBERSTONE PARK

Wadkins Eng.

Sta.

L & N.E.

Station

S6

BUSHBY

July 14th 1941 10 H.E.Bombs

SPINNEY HILL PARK

Steels & Busks Engineering

Water Works (Reservoir)

December 1940

THURNBY

Standard Eng.

John Bull Rubber

Chemical Works

Hospital

November 20th 1940

D7

D2

N3

EVINGTON

VICTORIA PARK

Rockets

X

U.S. 82nd Airborne camps 504th Parachute Infantry Reg.

X

L5

Potential flight path of the Fearless Fosdick see index.

London Road

Q6

STOUGHTON

P2

P3

Gartree Road

September 14th 1940

Military camp

LEICESTER EAST AIRFIELD

KNIGHTON

Welford Road

September 14th 1940

KNIGHTON PARK

U.S. 82nd Airborne billets 80th Anti-Tank Batt.

OADBY

July 30th 1942

LITTLE STRETTON

Leicester Race Course

STRETTON MAGNA

December 5th 1940

Stretton Hall Hospital

X

9th 41

Exploding Type July 30th 1942

WIGSTON

Golf Course

A6

April 1941

Newton Lane

0   1 mile

Gas Works

December 1940

GREAT GLEN

T.C.C. Publications ©2002

SOUTH EAST LEICESTER

MARCH 1944
U.S.A.A.F. Photograph.

▲ **VICTORIA PARK:** 'Z' Rockets

▲ **EVINGTON:** Tented U.S. Camps

▲ **OADBY:** U.S. Billets + Dakotas

▼ **BEEBY:** Starfish

▼ **SCRAPTOFT:** Tented U.S. Camp

▼ **NEWTON HARCOURT:** Starfish

This remarkable photograph, taken at the height of preparations for the D-Day landings was recently found at the National Archives, Maryland, U.S.A. Our map on page 10 & 11 provides an excellent key.

Can you spot the formation of 3 Dakotas near Oadby Racecourse?

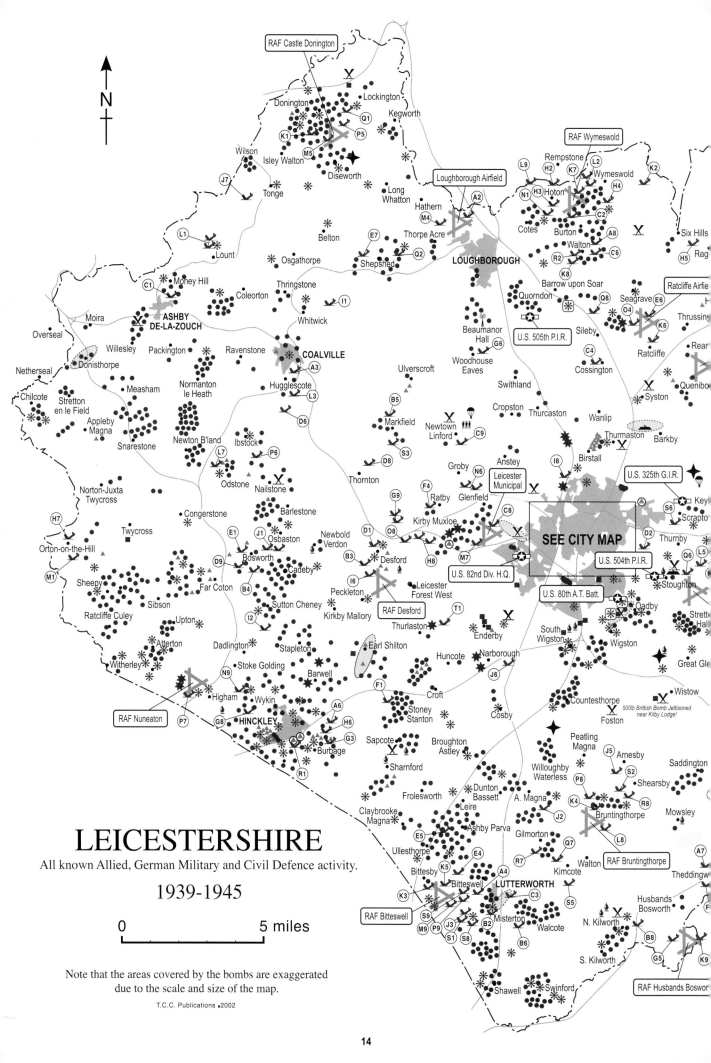

LEICESTERSHIRE

All known Allied, German Military and Civil Defence activity.

1939-1945

0   5 miles

Note that the areas covered by the bombs are exaggerated
due to the scale and size of the map.

T.C.C. Publications •2002

14

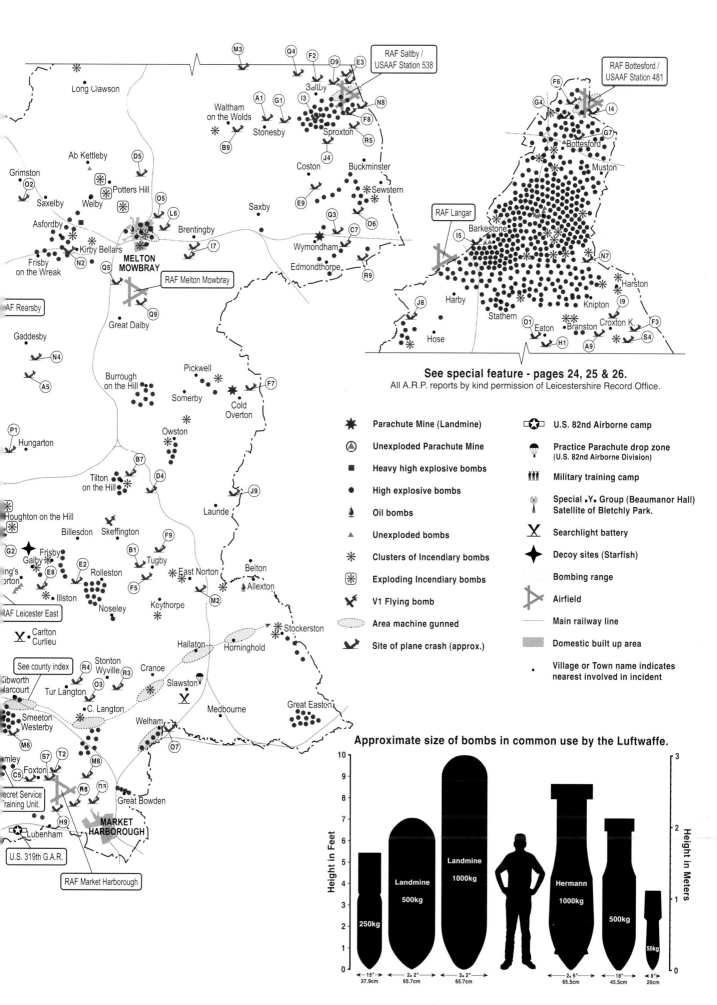

15

CITY MAP INDEX

Luftmine - Parachute mine (commonly known as Landmine)

Landmines came in two sizes, 1000kg & 500kg. Initially used to mine the sea and estuaries they were dropped by parachute to provide a soft entry. However, they also carried a "self destruction" fuse which was activated if it fell on land. These fuses with a time clock fitted, would be activated on impact and would run for approximately 20 seconds before exploding. (Many Olympic records must have been broken by the brave disposal teams who had to stop the clock or run 250 meters. Before this happened!). Filled with slow burning explosives these weapons created a tremendous blast wave which could last up to ten seconds. It would appear that in most cases this blast was channelled into a cone; devastating some areas, leaving others intact. Sometimes incendiary bombs were strapped to the outer casing to be distributed by the explosion. The 500kg mine was sometimes dropped in pairs.

	Grove Road I-4	Temple Road J-25	Tollemache Ave. C-17	Newstead Road P-22	Bannerman Road L-23	Victoria Park L-20	Frank Street H-22
DAMAGE	Frederick Road Mount Road Sherrard Road Vulcan Road	Copdale Road Crown Hills Avenue Elizabeth Street The Circle	Abbey Lane Downham Avenue Egerton Avenue Sudely Avenue	Knighton Drive Knighton Road Ratcliffe Road	Evington Valley Road Hollington Road area *One of a pair of 500kg one failed to explode.*	The Pavilion Granville Road Mayfield Road	Uppingham Road Spinney Hill Road

High Explosive Bombs

It would appear, on looking at Luftwaffe intelligence reports of aircraft active on the night of November 19th 1940, a common bomb load for aircraft was 1x250kg, 1x500kg and 1x250kg delayed action bomb (these delayed action bombs could be set to explode anywhere between 30 minutes to 72 hours after impact). Sometimes they also included a 250kg flammbome (a crude version of the present day napalm bomb) or 3x250kg and 1x250kg delayed action bomb. Most aircraft appear to have included a delayed action bomb in their payload. For example, a Luftflotte 3 Junker 88, carrying a trainee crew, aiming for the London Road Railway Station dropped 1x250kg, 1x500kg and 1x250kg delayed action bomb. This incident caused the highest number of casualties during the raid (41 fatal). The bombs fell on the corner of Highfields Street/ Upper Titchbourne Street; the delayed action bomb fell in Upper Titchbourne Street and was successfully removed. The Luftwaffe crew reported that they had not observed the result of their bombing run.

Albion St.	K-19	Clock Tower.	I-18	Forest Rd.	G-22	Knighton Park Rd.	M-21	Rutland St.	I-19	St.Peters Rd.	K-22
Alexander St.	J-15	Cobden St.	G-21	Fosse Rd. South.	K-15	Knighton Rd.	O-21	Saffron Hill Rd.	P-17	Stonesby Ave.	V-18
Allendal Rd.	N-24	Conduit St.	J-20	Frank St.	H-22	Latimer St.	K-15	Saffron Road.	W-17	Stoughton St.	K-21
Ash St.	G-22	Constitution Hill.	J-20	Gravel St.	H-18	Leamington St.	K-15	Samuel St.	H-20	Suffolk St.	I-20
Bannerman Rd.	L-23	Cricket Gnd.	M-17	Great Central St.	I-16	Livingstone St.	K-15	Saville St.	J-24	Titchbourne St.	K-20
Beech St.	G-22	Cort Crescent.	K-10	Green Lane Rd.	I-24	London Rd.	N-22	Saxby St.	K-20	Trinity Hosp. Gnds.	K-17
Bolsover St.	J-24	Cranmer St.	K-15	Guthlaxton St.	K-21	Melbourne Rd.	J-21	Severn St.	K-20	Waterloo St.	K-19
Bolton St.	J-14	Dover St.	K-19	Gwendolen Rd.	K-24	Mere Rd.	K-22	Shirley Rd.	Q-22	Webster Rd.	K-9
Bradbourne Rd.	K-23	East Park Rd.	J-22	Hastings St	K-19	Mill Hill Lane.	K-22	Slate St.	J-20	Wellington St.	K-19
Briton St.	K-15	East Short St.	J-20	Highfields St.	K-19	Newarke St.	K-17	South Albion St.	K-19	Western Rd.	L-16
Brunswick St.	G-20	East St.	J-20	Hobart St.	K-20	Norwood Rd.	L-24	Southampton St.	I-19	Wigston Rd.	T-27
Calais St.	K-19	Elmfield Ave.	M-22	Holmfield Ave.	N-23	Peel St.	J-20	Sparkenhoe St.	K-21	Willow St.	G-20
Campbell St.	J-19	Essex Rd.	O-25	Humberstone Rd.	H-21	Prestwold Rd.	G-22	Spinney Hill Park.	J-22	Worthington St.	J-22
Carrington St.	J-20	Evington St.	K-20	Ireton Rd.	D-25	Queen St.	I-20	St.Albans St.	L-21	Unity Ave.	G-22
Carisbrooke Rd.	Q-22	Evington Valley Rd.	K-23	Kimberly Rd.	M-23	Quenby St.	G-23	St.Ives Rd.	D-25	Up. Brown St.	J-18
Cattle Market.	N-18	Fairfield St.	J-22	King St.	K-18	Ridley St.	K-15	St.Margarets Sta.	H-18	Up. Tichbourne St.	K-20
Cavendish Rd.	P-17	Filbert St.	M-16	Kitchener Road.	I-24	Roman St.	K-15	St.Marys Rd.	M-21		

Incendiary Bombs

Principal bombs used were 1 or 2kg Magnesium bombs, which varied in design - some, in order to deter fire fighters, were fitted with explosive charges, timed to explode 5-7 minutes after impact. I remember we 9 year olds being taught, at school, how to deal with these bombs with stirrup pumps, dustbin lids and sandbags. I'm glad I didn't have to put this to the test! These Incendiary bombs were dropped in containers, designed to explode at a given height to give a good spread, containing anything from 10 - 600 bombs. The exploding type were reported at Oadby Racecourse, Spinney Hill, and the Filbert Street areas. Some much larger oil/phosphorous filled bombs (Oil bombs/Flammbome) were also used.

Damage Reported (cause undetermined: bomb, blast or firebomb.)

Aberdale Rd.	S-20	Belgrave Av.	C-19	Cross St.	E-20	Myrtle Rd.	K-20	Regents Rd.	J-19	Thurcaston Rd.	A-18
Abingdon Rd.	L-21	Birstall Rd.	A-18	Derwent St.	J-21	Nansen Rd.	J-25	Rutland St.	I-19	Shirley St.	C-19
Allington St.	F-21	Blunts La.	J-16	Gipsy Lane.	D-24	Newpark St.	J-22	Scraptoft La.	G-26	Vann St.	C-19
Aylestone Rd.	I-11	Carisbrooke Ave.	Q-22	Grasmere St.	M-16	New Walk.	J-19	Skipworth St.	K-20	Warling St.	J-20
Babington Row.	S-20	Cedar Rd.	K-20	Hollington Rd.	K-22	Northampton Sq.	J-19	Slawston St.	J-19	Wellington St.	J-19
Baker St.	I-19	Checketts Rd.	C-20	Lincoln St.	J-20	Osmaston Rd.	K-22	Springfield Rd.	N-21		
Bardolf St.	F-20	Chester St.	I-21	Medway St.	K-20	Prebend St.	K-20	Tewkesbury St.	I-15		

Unexploded Bombs 30 U.X.B's were reported on the 19th November.

Applegate St.	Next to the Talbut Inn.	J-17	8 Knighton Rise	Garden.	P-24
Bede Island	Canal / river?	L-16	London Rd.	Pavement.	M-21
Cobden St.	Premises.	G-21	209 Mere Rd.	Pavement, front of house	
Dover St.	Premises.	K-19		(Herman).	J-21
Earlhouse St.	Roadway.	J-20	Mere Rd.	Near Spinney Hill Park.	
Evington Dr.	Pavement.	L-25		(Herman).	J-21
2 Fitzroy St.	Premises.	J-15	1 Mervin Rd.	Garden. (Landmine).	O-22
Fox St.	Rail yard.	J-19	Mill St. - Welford Rd.	Roadway.	K-18
Gt. Central St.	Printing wks.	I-17	Queen St.	Grain warehouse – Yard.	L-23
High Cross St.	Roadway.	I-17	1 Southernay Rd.	Garden. (Landmine).	O-22
Humberstone	Near Village Church	F-28	Town Hall	Basement.	J-18
John Bull Rubber	Yard.	K-24	2a Twycross St.	Premises.	I-20
Kirby Muxloe	Gullett La.Bridge (Landmine)		32 Upp. Tichbourne St.	Garden.	K-20

Searchlight & A.A. Batteries

These batteries were in some cases mobile. Some eventually had light twin Lewis machine guns. The 'Z' Rockets based on Victoria Park were anti-aircraft rockets, carried in racks of sixteen. 262 were on the park for a short time and were replaced with wooden dummy rockets. None were fired in anger, but both Western Park (14/11/40) and Wigston-Oadby (19/11/40) sites were machine-gunned by enemy aircraft.

Major Fires 55 fires were reported on the night of 19/20th November 1940.

J. Vines & Co., Calais St.   **Prov. Baptist Chapel**, Newarke St.   **Freeman Hardy & Willis**, Rutland St
Browetts Garage, Dover St.   **Grieves & Co.**, Queen St..   **Lulhams Warehouse**, Northampton Sq.
Kemp & Co. Ltd., Dover St.   **Faire Brothers**, Rutland St.
Hearth & Co., Newarke St.   **Tigers Rugby Ground**, Welford Rd.

Summary: 122 people died and 284 were injured in the city raids. 255 houses destroyed, almost 6,000 damaged (to varying degrees). 56 factories destroyed, 277 damaged. One school destroyed. 55 fires were reported. An estimated 12-16,000 people made homeless and £1,000,000 damage (1940s prices). 223 air raid warnings were sounded during the course of the war. The new tonnage of bombs found would suggest that up to 40 German aircraft attacked the city and county on the 19th November 1940. Tonnage of bombs would total approximately 40 tons. The Luftwaffe considered 50 tons and over as a major raid. In the county 24 civilians died and 77 were injured and a minimum of 265 airman died and 94 injured.

County Map Index Summary

On the map in this book are plotted the approximate location of 1,415 High Explosives and thousands of incendiary bombs. Thankfully most of these bombs fell on open farmland and apart from damage to livestock, barns and crops, little damage was done. Listed below are incidents where casualties and damage to property occurred and other notable incidents not featured on other pages of the book.

Location	Date	Description
Ab Kettleby	3.10.40	An unexploded 1800kg 'Satan' bomb aimed for Holwell Iron Works, was recovered and disarmed.
Appleby Magna	4.12.40	1000kg U.X.B. fell 200 yds. at rear of Morris Arms.
Barrow-upon-Soar	23.8.42	Explosive Incendiaries on Foxhill farm - fire damage to farmhouse and buildings.
Birstall	Nov-40	10 U.X.B.'s fell adjacent to the River Soar. Despite many attempts to extricate them they were abandoned due to their situation below the water table. No precise location was recorded.
Braunstone	10.1.42	500kg H.E. bomb fell in fields 150 yds. from Turnbull Drive, causing blast damage to 207 houses. This lone Dornier, out on a special operation against special targets, was later intercepted by a Beaufighter and after jettisoning it's remaining bomb over Twycross it crashed near Nuneaton. The crew of 3 bailed out and were taken prisoner.
Burbage	2.10.40	Incendiaries and H.E.'s caused serious damage to 2 houses - no casualties.
Burbage	17.5.41	H.E.'s damaged 8 houses beyond repair and caused minor damage to nearby houses. H.E.'s also fell on 2 houses along Sapcote Road causing minor damage.
Burton-on-the-Wolds	23.8.42	H.E.'s blew out windows of a wooden bungalow and Glovers farm at 10.59pm.
Coalville	28.8.40	H.E.'s straddled rail line and caused damage to 3 houses along London Road at 11.00pm.
Coalville	29.6.42	An 1800kg unexploded 'Satan' bomb was recovered from Owen Street and removed by the Bomb Disposal Service. It was originally dropped on 15/12/40.
Countesthorpe	10.4.41	18 H.E.'s fell over village causing blast damage to 100 houses, with severe blast damage to 3 houses.
Donisthorpe	3.8.42	At 2.02pm a lone Luftwaffe plane machine-gunned streets and dropped 4 H.E.'s on Donisthorpe, causing blast damage to 120 houses. One bomb bounced off the road over the 'Caves Arms' public house (with 20 customers) and landed in the adjacent colliery workshops. A cottage was destroyed along with colliery workshops. 1 adult died, 4 seriously injured and 10 with slight injuries.
Dunton Bassett	25.8.40	H.E.'s and Incendiaries caused damage to 2 houses. 1 seriously injured. (1st bombs to fall on county.)
Earl Shilton	1940	Luftwaffe plane machine-gunned Keats Lane area. There were no casualties.
Great Easton	4.2.41	9 H.E.'s caused damage to Bringhurst School windows and the road between villages were blocked.
Higham-on-the-Hill	25.6.42	Incendiaries torched nearby disused railway station.
Hinckley	26.6.40	Incendiaries torched Alms House and H.E.'s fell in rural areas.
Hinckley	4.12.40	5 H.E.'s caused serious damage to 5 houses. Casualties: 1 injured.
Hinckley	30.7.42	Incendiaries fell on Coventry Road, Thirlmere Road, Beaumont Avenue, Nutts Lane, London Road, King George's Way, Barwell Lane, Trinity Vicarage Road and William Iliffe Street. Casualties: 1 woman died.
Houghton-on-the-Hill	4.2.41	300 Explosive Incendiaries dropped outside village.
Houghton-on-the-Hill	15.3.41	12 H.E.'s straddled village. 3 H.E.'s landed on village damaging 30 houses, 3 later had to be demolished. Casualties: 9 injured, 4 of them minor.
Kegworth	28.8.40	Considerable damage caused to houses, gas and water mains. The road between Kegworth and Hathern was also blocked. Casualties: 1 died.
Kibworth	22.9.40	At 4.30pm one Luftwaffe plane machine-gunned Kibworth from a low altitude and proceeded in the direction of East Langton by Hallaton to Horninghold finding machine-gun targets on the way in the shape of motorists, cyclists and blackberry-pickers. This episode followed an unsuccessful attempt by the raider to bomb the L.M.S. Railway near East Langton. There were no casualties.
Loughborough	13.8.41	4 H.E.'s fell between Parklands Drive and Beacon Road at 12.55am, causing slight damage to 9 houses. Casualties: 1 minor injury.
Lutterworth	31.7.42	At 2.45pm one Luftwaffe plane machine-gunned the town causing minor damage to house property.
Markfield	13.8.41	A 500kg H.E. fell in fields causing minor damage to 2 nearby houses, at 1.15am.
Nailstone	23.12.40	1 H.E. bomb badly damaged a house on the Hinckley - Ibstock Road. An unexploded H.E. was recovered from Hollow farm fields.
Noseley	4.2.41	1 H.E. bomb fell near Noseley Hall. Windows in the village hall, church and mansion were blown out.
Packington	4.1.41	7 H.E.'s fell between Breach farm and Farm town, straddling railway line.
Packington	12.3.41	1 H.E. fell on Hall farm damaging a Tractor. Another H.E. fell on Yew Tree farm causing damage to roof tiles and windows.
Queniborough	28.8.40	H.E.'s rendered a number of houses uninhabitable. One time delayed H.E. exploded 4 hours later. Casualties: 2 injured.
Sewstern	9.9.40	H.E. bomb fell on edge of ironstone quarry, causing damage to equipment and machinery.
South Wigston	14.9.40	Incendiaries fell in yard of Bassett Street School, no's 25 & 50 Clifford Street and Modern School grounds.
Thurmaston	10.4.41	H.E.'s and Incendiaries damaged 100 houses with broken windows, doors and displaced roof tiles.
Tilton-on-the-Hill	23.1.44	At 9.30am a U.S. lorry, travelling through the village with a load comprising of 19 x 500lb bombs, over-turned and demolished a wall. Fortunately the bombs did not explode and there were no casualties.
Welham	Nov-40	1 H.E. bomb. Railway sidings machine-gunned causing damage to wires and windows of signal box.
Wigston	Dec-40	12 H.E.'s caused damage to house. Slight injuries to the occupant.
Wigston	30.7.42	Over 100 exploding Incendiaries fell on the Grange Orchard off Leicester Road.
Willesley	Nov-40	4 H.E.'s hit Searchlight battery. Casualties: 1 died, 2 injured.
Wilson	15.1.41	6 Time delayed H.E.'s fell in fields south of village, causing damage to a chimney. Casualties: 1 soldier in a state of shock.

Blast Damage = Displaced tiles, doors and broken windows

Severe Blast Damage = Structural damage to buildings.

NOTE: Countesthorpe, Queniborough and Houghton were bombed possibly due to local searchlight activity.

Luftmine - Parachute mines

Barwell	Nov-40	2 Parachute Mines caused slight damage to houses.
Birstall	14.11.40	2 Parachute Mines caused widespread damage as far as Rothley. Windows of Thurmaston W.M.C. blown out.
Cold Overton	1940	Parachute mine. No damage reported.
Higham-on-the-Hill	15.11.40	2 Parachute Mines fell on Rowden House farm causing damage to windows. No casualties.
Hinckley	15.1.40	2 unexploded Parachute Mines fell on open ground near L.M.S. Railway Station.
Kirby Muxloe	19.11.40	3 Parachute Mines See page 29.
Narborough	Nov-40	2 Parachute Mines fell between Narborough and Huncote causing much damage to windows and plaster at Huncote Post Office and Enderby village.
Sileby	Nov-40	Parachute Mine fell near Quebec farm causing minor damage.
Thurlaston	Nov-40	Parachute Mine causes damage to water supply to Enderby Co-op Society's farm. No casualties.
Wymondham	Nov 40	Parachute mine. No damage reported.

Airfields

'Swampys'/Environmentalists would have had serious nervous breakdowns during the war. Vast amounts of land were requisitioned by the Air Ministry to build almost 700 airfields throughout the U.K. Each estimated to cost up to £500,000 (1940's prices.) These requisitions happened almost overnight. Objections were dismissed out of hand. There were 5 airstrips in Leicestershire in 1939. These were improved and others constructed to bring the total to 14. Note the extent of the area covered by ammunition, fuel and supply dumps, etc. Most of the airfields are clearly depicted within this book by reconnaisance photographs taken before and during the war. However, the missing ones (no suitable photo's available) are clearly represented on the county map (pages 14 & 15): R.A.F. Bitteswell, Ratcliffe, R.A.F. Rearsby and R.A.F. Wymeswold.

Civil Defence bomb plot map

This map, displayed in the armoury of Beaumanor Hall, was found to have many pins missing. Although it was comparatively easy to identify where the original pins were embedded we had no idea of the colour of the pin used to denote the type of bomb plotted, i.e. red for I.B.'s and blue for H.E.'s. Fortunately we have since found detailed A.R.P. reports which have enabled us to identify these. For the purpose of the book cover, we have reconstructed the map to resemble the original as it was in 1945. Please bare in mind that due to scale and the difficulty of plotting bombs which fell on open land, the Civil Defence plotters appear to have grouped bombs in clusters rather than staggered lines (which would normally be the case), to avoid covering place names. For the purpose of my own maps I have adjusted some of the bomb positions (with the help of eyewitnesses), accordingly.

CENSORSHIP

Rigid censorship was essential during the war, mainly for national security and protection of our armed forces. Great care was taken to ensure that any news item which could help the enemy in any small way was suppressed. For example, although many people saw landmines floating down on parachutes, the existence of these weapons was never acknowledged by the M.O.D. until late in the war in order to hide the fact that many failed to explode due to being snagged on buildings/trees etc. they were rarely mentioned in news or A.R.P.reports (if the enemy had known this he would have altered the fuses and detonators).

Another area of censorship existed for the protection of morale and avoid inflicting unnecessary emotional stress on the population. The golden rule not to report any fatalities or serious events until all next-of-kin had been informed was strictly enforced and any such report was always concluded by the statement "next-of-kin have been informed". Young readers may find the above strict safeguards rather odd, as sadly, these responsible and necessary precautions appear to be lacking in today's obsessive quest to provide instant and alarmist "on the spot" news reports.

AIRCRAFT CRASHES

On the following pages are listed details of most of the aircraft which crashed in Leicestershire during the period 1939-45. This list does not include aircraft which crashed (there were many) on or within the perimeter of the airfields. Due to the censorship rules it has been difficult to obtain exact details of casualties and locations, A.R.P. reports were very brief and only gave the barest details, most could not name the type of aircraft or be sure of the number of casualties. However, although extra information has been extracted from other sources, I doubt if the full casualty figures are complete.

	Date	Aircraft Type	Crash Location	Fatal	Injured
A1	22.9.39	Hereford	Nr. Stonesby.	-	-
A2	17.11.39	Hawker Hart	Nr. Loughborough.	-	-
A3	17.11.39	Hawker Audax	Nr. Coalville Grammer School.	-	-
A4	4.1.40	Hawker Hart	Nr. Lutterworth.	-	-
A5	17.1.40	Hawker Hind	Nr. Barsby.	-	-
A6	21.3.40	Miles Mentor	Burbage Wood, Burbage.	-	-
A7	29.3.40	Hawker Hart	Nr. Theddingworth.	-	-
A8	15.4.40	Harvard	Nr. Walton-on-the-Wolds. PBO	-	-
A9	30.4.40	Hampden	Nr. Croxton Kerrial.	4	-
B1	9.5.40	Hereford	Nr. Tugby.	-	-
B2	11.6.40	Oxford	Nr. Lutterworth.	-	-
B3	27.6.40	Tiger Moth	Nr. Desford. PBO	-	-
B4	28.8.40	Defiant	Nr. Market Bosworth.	-	-
B5	28.8.40	Tiger Moth	Nr. Markfield.	-	-
B6	29.9.40	Hurricane	Rugby Co-op farm, Misterton.	-	-
B7	8.10.40	Hawker Hart	Nr. Tilton-on-the-Hill.	1	-
B8	14.10.40	Anson	Nr. North Kilworth.	-	3
B9	16.10.40	Tiger Moth	Nr. Waltham-on-the-Wolds.	-	-
C1	3.11.40	Puss Moth	Nr. Ashby-de-la-Zouch.	-	-
C2	14.11.40	Dornier Do 17Z-3	Nr. School, Burton-on-the-Wolds.	4	-
C3	21.11.40	Hampden	Nr. Lutterworth.	-	-
C4	21.12.40	Fairey Battle	Nr. Cossington.	1	-
C5	22.12.40	Blenheim	Half a mile SW of Foxton.	-	-
C6	23.2.41	Defiant	Nr. Walton-on-the-Wolds. CBO	-	-
C7	21.3.41	Manchester	Nr. Wymondham.	4	2
C8	27.3.41	Tiger Moth	Nr. Braunstone Aerodrome.	-	-
C9	8.4.41	Tiger Moth	Nr. Newtown Linford. PBO	-	-
D1	9.4.41	Heinkel He 111	Roe's Rest Farm, Desford.	-	2
D2	10.4.41	Hampden	St. Denys Road, Evington. CK	3	1
D3	20.5.41	Wellington	Nr. Market Harborough.	-	-
D4	28.5.41	Wellington	Colborough Hill, Halstead.	5	1
D5	11.6.41	Fairey Battle	Nr. Barton Lodge, Melton.	-	-
D6	19.6.41	Tiger Moth	Nr. Ellistown, Coalville. PBO	-	-
D7	25.6.41	Oxford	Linden Drive, Evington, trying to force land on Golf Course.	-	-
D8	2.8.41	Tiger Moth	Nr. Thornton.	-	-
D9	15.8.41	Tiger Moth	Nr. Market Bosworth.	-	-
E1	25.8.41	Tiger Moth	Nr. Market Bosworth.	-	-
E2	12.9.41	Hampden	Barn Farm, Nr. Rolleston.	2	4
E3	12.9.41	Hampden's	Collided over Saltby airfield. Both crashed nearby.	8	-
	17.9.41	Tiger Moth	Nunnery Farm, Leicester.	-	-
E4	29.9.41	Wellington	Nr. Bitteswell.	7	1
E5	23.10.41	Wellington	Nr. Ullesthorpe.	-	-
E6	25.10.41	Hampden	Between Ratcliffe and Seagrave.	-	-
E7	16.11.41	Oxford	Nr. Shepshed.	-	-
E8	22.11.41	Miles Master	Nr. Illston-on-the-Hill.	-	-
E9	9.12.41	Hampden	North of Wymondham.	2	-
F1	26.12.41	Oxford	Nr. Stoney Stanton.	-	-
F2	10.2.42	Hampden	Nr. Saltby.	-	-
F3	8.3.42	Hampden	East of Croxton Kerrial.	2	2
F4	13.3.42	Blenheim	Nr. Ratby.	-	-
F5	30.3.42	Allied Aircraft	1 mile from Tugby Church.	-	-
F6	8.4.42	Lancaster	N-S boundary road of Bottesford airfield.	-	5
F7	19.4.42	Oxford	Stone House, Cold Overton.	1	-
F8	2.5.42	Hampden	Nr. Saltby Airfield.	-	-
F9	2.5.42	Blenheim	Tugby Wood, A47.	3	-
G1	5.5.42	Hampden	Nr. Stonesby.	-	4
G2	9.6.42	Blenheim	In trees near Houghton-on-the-Hill.	2	-
G3	14.6.42	Oxford	1.5 miles East of Hinckley.	5	-
G4	19.8.42	Lancaster	Normanton. Nr. Bottesford.	6	-
G5	28.8.42	Miles Master	Nr. H. Bosworth Airfield.	-	-
G6	7.10.42	Wellington	Nr. Woodhouse Eaves.	5	-
G7	19.10.42	Hurricane	Nr. Bottesford. PBO	-	-
G8	8.11.42	Wellington	Nr. Hinckley.	-	-
G9	14.11.42	Tiger Moth's	Botcheston, Nr. Desford.	2	-
H1	25.11.42	Allied Aircraft	Nr. Eaton, Waltham-on-the-Wolds.	-	-
H2	28.11.42	Wellington	Half a mile North of Hoton.	2	-
H3	6.12.42	Wellington	350 yards South of Hoton.	2	2
H4	11.12.42	Wellington	Nr. Wymeswold Airfield.	1	-
H5	12.12.42	British Aircraft	Between Six Hills and Ragdale.	-	-
H6	10.1.43	Wellington	Nr. Lutterworth Rd, Burbage.	1	2
H7	15.1.43	Wellington	Nr. Orton-on-the-Hill.	1	-
H8	1.2.43	Thunderbolt's	Collided over Park House Farm and New Bridge Farm, Kirby Muxloe.	2	-
H9	7.2.43	Wellington	Nr. Mkt. Harborough Airfield CBO	-	-
I1	15.2.43	Wellington	Hermitage Farm Nr. Blackbrook Res.	5	-
I2	16.2.43	Tiger Moth	Between Sutton and Dadlington.	2	-
I3	17.2.43	Wellington	1 mile NW of Sproxton.	4	-
I4	18.2.43	Lancaster	Nr. Bottesford Airfield.	7	-
I5	5.3.43	Allied Aircraft	West of Plungar.	-	-
I6	9.3.43	Tiger Moth	Nr. Desford.	-	-
I7	8.4.43	Lancaster & Oxford	Collision between Brentingby and Burton Lazars.	9	-
I8	25.4.43	Wellington	Stocking Farm, Beaumont Leys, site nr. Blenheim Way.	-	-
I9	6.5.43	Blenheim	Nr. Croxton Kerrial.	-	-
J1	8.6.43	Tiger Moth	Collided with another plane and crashed Nr. Market Bosworth.	-	-
J2	26.6.43	Wellington	Crashed between Gilmorton and Ashby Magna.	-	5
J3	29.6.43	Wellington	Nr. Glebe Farm, Lutterworth.	-	-
J4	3.7.43	Wellington	3/4 mile South of Sproxton.	-	-
J5	23.7.43	Tomahawk	Caught fire and PBO over Arnesby.	-	1
J6	27.7.43	Oxford	Nr. Whetstone.	1	-
J7	2.8.43	Wellington	Nr. Breedon-on-the-Hill. CBO	-	-
J8	3.8.43	Wellington	1 Mile NW of Hose.	-	-
J9	5.8.43	Beaufighter	Withcote Lodge, Launde.	2	-
K1	7.8.43	Wellington	Nr. Castle Donington.	5	-
K2	17.8.43	Halifax	2 miles East of Wymeswold.	-	-
K3	17.8.43	Wellington	Nr. Bitteswell Airfield.	-	-
K4	21.8.43	Wellington	The Firs, Bruntingthorpe.	-	-
K5	6.9.43	Wellington	Nr. Bitteswell.	-	-
K6	6.9.43	Tiger Moth	Nr. Ratcliffe. PBO	-	-
K7	8.9.43	Lancaster	Nr. Wymeswold.	9	-
K8	25.9.43	Wellington	Nr. Walton-on-the-Wolds.	5	-
K9	26.9.43	Wellington	Nr. Husbands Bosworth Airfield.	4	1
L1	3.10.43	British Aircraft	Nr. Lount, Staunton Harold.	1	1
L2	3.10.43	Spitfire's	Nr. Wymeswold.	1	1
L3	14.10.43	Mosquito	Elliston Farm, Coalville.	2	-
L4	22.10.43	Wellington	Nr. The Bell Inn, Gumley.	5	-
L5	5.11.43	Oxford	Between Stoughton and Houghton.	-	2
L6	31.12.43	Anson	Saxby Road, 1 mile E of Melton.	-	-
L7	28.1.44	Wellington	Barn Farm, Odstone.	1	4

ID	Date	Aircraft	Location	A	B
L8	28.1.44	Wellington	Nr. Bruntingthorpe.	-	-
L9	3.2.44	Wellington	Sims Farm, NW of Hoton.	-	-
M1	11.2.44	Wellington	Back of Church, Orton-on-the-Hill.	-	1
M2	13.2.44	Flying Fortress	1 mile SE of East Norton Church.	-	1
M3	13.2.44	Tiger Moth	Road junction of Branston, Melton and Grantham.	-	-
M4	19.2.44	Boston	Dishley Bridge, Derby Road, Loughborough.	-	-
M5	25.2.44	Allied Aircraft	Nr. Castle Donington. CBO	-	-
M6	11.3.44	Oxford	Nr. Smeeton Westerby.	3	-
M7	20.3.44	Miles Master	Nr. Braunstone Aerodrome.	-	1
M8	27.3.44	Wellington	Nr. Market Harborough Airfield.	5	-
M9	11.4.44	Martinet	Nr. Bitteswell Airfield.	-	2
N1	23.4.44	Allied Aircraft	Field opp. Prestwold Woodyard.	-	-
N2	1.5.44	Beaufighter	West Kirby Bellars Nr. Main Road.	2	-
N3	5.5.44	Blenheim	Nr. Houghton-on-the-Hill.	-	-
N4	13.5.44	Oxford	1.5 miles SE of Gaddesby.	5	-
N5	14.5.44	Auster	During a public display outside Abbey Park boundary.	1	-
N6	27.5.44	Tiger Moth's	1.5 miles SE of Groby.	-	-
N7	7.6.44	Lancaster	Belvoir Woods Nr. Belvoir Castle.	6	1
N8	7.6.44	Short Stirling	Nr. Saltby Airfield.	-	-
N9	18.6.44	Wellington	Phillips Farm, Wykin.	-	3
O1	11.7.44	Lancaster	Rail Sidings 200 yds. W of Eaton.	6	-
O2	17.7.44	Wellington	Between Saxelby and Ragdale.	5	-
O3	1.8.44	Wellington	In field half mile NNE of Church Langton.	-	5
O4	7.8.44	Spitfire	Nr. Ratcliffe Aerodrome.	1	-
O5	13.8.44	Wellington	Thorpe Road, Melton.	7	1
O6	19.8.44	Blenheim	Sewstern Grange, Wymondham.	1	-
O7	30.8.44	Wellington	Nr. Rail Sidings SE of Welham.	5	1
O8	7.9.44	Norseman	300 yards East of Desford Junction Signal Box.	2	-
O9	7.9.44	Hurricane	Nr. Saltby Airfield.	-	-
P1	8.9.44	Wellington	Cemetery Road between Keyham and Hungarton.	8	-
P2	11.9.44	Fearless Fosdick			

This U.S. Flying Fortress, badly damaged in a daylight raid on a synthetic oil plant, caught fire in mid air whilst trying to return to it's base. The crew baled out between Peterborough and Corby thinking it would fall in open country but it remained in flight on a course which would take it over the centre of Leicester. It crashed near Stoughton Airfield, on Cotterill Spinney. If it had remained in flight for another 20-40 seconds it would have crashed somewhere in the city centre, full of unsuspecting city workers.

A minimum of 265 airman lost their lives and 94 were injured in Leicestershire
PBO = Pilot Baled Out.   **CBO** = Crew Baled Out.   **CK** = Civilian Killed.

ID	Date	Aircraft	Location	A	B
P3	15.9.44	Thunderbolt	Dovedale Road, Stoneygate, Leicester. CK	2	-
P4	21.9.44	Wellington	Nr. Theddingworth.	-	-
P5	22.9.44	Oxford	Nr. Castle Donington Airfield.	-	-
P6	27.9.44	Flying Fortress	Between Nailstone and Ibstock.	9	-
P7	13.10.44	Wellington	Railway next to Nuneaton Airfield.	-	-
P8	15.10.44	Wellington	Nr. Bruntingthorpe.	-	-
P9	17.10.44	Wellington	Nr. Bitteswell Airfield.	-	-
Q1	19.10.44	Wellington	Nr. Castle Donington Airfield.	6	1
Q2	28.10.44	Thunderbolt	Nr. Shepshed.	1	-
Q3	7.11.44	Oxford	Nr. Wymondham.	4	-
Q4	27.11.44	Lancaster	Between Croxton Kerrial & Saltby.	3	4
Q5	30.11.44	Mosquito	Nr. Melton Mowbray Airfield.	1	1
Q6	1944	Stirling	Avoiding collision with a Horsa Glider. Clarks Bush, Stoughton.		
Q7	5.1.45	Wellington	Nr. Kimcote.	4	1
Q8	10.1.45	Dakota	Between Barrow and Sileby.	3	-
Q9	14.1.45	Short Stirling	Nr. Melton Mowbray.	-	-
R1	15.1.45	Wellington	Holt Farm, Sketchley.	6	-
R2	17.1.45	Wellington	Nr. Walton-on-the-Wolds.	6	-
R3	20.1.45	Spitfire	Nr. Stonton Wyville. PBO		
R4	20.1.45	Flying Fortress	Nr. Tur Langton. CBO	-	2
R5	22.1.45	Flying Fortress	Buckminster-Saltby area.	-	3
R6	3.2.45	Wellington	Nr. Market Harborough.		
R7	7.2.45	Wellington	Nr. Gilmorton.		
R8	11.2.45	Wellington	Nr. Shearsby.		
R9	24.2.45	Halifax	Woodwell Spinney, Drift Road, Edmondthorpe.	7	-
S1	4.3.45	Flying Fortress	100 yards from Moorbarns Farm, Lutterworth. CBO	-	-
S2	4.3.45	Wellington	Nr. Shearsby.		
S3	21.3.45	Tiger Moth	Nr. Markfield.		
S4	25.3.45	Flying Fortress	Nr. Croxton Kerrial. CBO over Saltby.		
S5	2.4.45	Wellington	500 yards East of Stanford Road, Kimcote.	7	1
S6	8.4.45	Lancaster	North of Station Lane, Thurnby Lodge, Scraptoft. (see page 28.)	7	-
S7	9.4.45	Lancaster	Damaged garden fence in Foxton.	7	-
S8	17.4.45	Flying Fortress	Sanders Farm, Moorbarns, Lutterworth. CBO	-	9
S9	17.4.45	Wellington	Nr. Bitteswell.	-	7
T1	25.4.45	Beaufort	Half a mile NE of Thurlaston off Enderby Road.	-	1
T2	4.5.45	Mosquito	Nr. Foxton.	2	-

R.A.F. Photo ©1945

BLABY: August 1945. Blaby Wharf Maintenance Unit 63, off Leicester Road looking south. The County Arms, top.

This R.A.F. Depot was formed to collect and recycle most of the aircraft which crashed in the county. The photograph above was taken just as it was being disbanded, but the tragic remains of many crashed aircraft can still be seen in the storage area (which were converted pig sties!).

COUNTY A.R.P. OFFICER'S REPORT

Since my last report which was dated 31st October, enemy activity in the County has been considerable.

Incendiary bombs have fallen at Narborough, Enderby, Sharnford, Sapcote, Osbaston, Swinford, Desford, Wellsborough, Congerstone, Oadby, Great Glen, Sheepy Magna, Allexton, and Sutton-in-the-Elms. A serious fire was caused at Stackley House, Great Glen; apart from this there was no appreciable damage.

High explosive bombs and parachute mines to the number of more than 200 have been dropped, and considerable material damage has been done, notably at Melton Mowbray and Kirby Muxloe, but the damage cannot be regarded as excessive when the total weight of explosives used is taken into account. Viewed in the same light, casualties have not been heavy although six persons were killed.

High explosive bombs were dropped at Welham, Enderby, Melton Mowbray (where machine-gunning also occurred) Birstall, Walcote, Cotesbach, Bottesford, Sharnford, Wellsborough, Cadeby, Twycross, Higham, Stretton, Swinford, Ashby Parva, Croft, Newbold Verdon, Kirby Muxloe, Sheepy Magna, Sileby, Kibworth, North Kilworth, Saddington, Wymondham, Bittesby, Willesley, Narborough, Shepshed, Lubenham, Edmondthorpe, Leicester Forest West, Quorn, Rolleston, Barwell, Thurlaston, Sewstern, Packington, and Asfordby.

The Mobile Canteens have been in operation in Leicester City, Coventry and Birmingham, also at Melton Mowbray, Kirby Muxloe and Asfordby, and have proved of the utmost value.

The W.V.S. has already made its worth apparent in Raid Welfare and no praise can be too high for the promptness and organisation which provided shelter and meals for some 300 people following the Kirby Muxloe raid.

Speaking generally, the bombing which has taken place has, in my opinion, in no way affected the determination of the public to hold on, but it is useless to deny that the nervousness of already nervous people has been increased, especially in the City and its immediate surroundings, and as a result of this, large numbers are trekking into the country districts at nightfall, usually by car, to find shelter where they may. Should this redistribution of the night population continue, and night bombing ensue, a strain will be thrown on the Services located in rural areas far beyond anything anticipated or so far experienced, and some movement of parties at night over considerable distances will be inevitable.

> W. T. DOWELL.
>
> County A.R.P. Officer.

28th November, 1940.

The paragraph in the above report relating to the general reaction of the public, shows how the authorities closely monitored morale during the war. It is noticeable that almost all A.R.P. reports on incidents involving loss of life or severe damage to property commented on the morale of the people in the area involved. I myself do not remember any of the families in my district leaving the city at night as the report suggests, but bearing in mind that most people living in my area did not possess cars, this is not surprising! I do remember the sudden disappearance of my evacuee friends after the November 19th raid who, I found out later, returned to London having considered that if they were to be bombed, they would rather it happen while at home, with their family!

NOTE: The above report does not include incidents which took place within the city boundary.

Leicester shows the way!

During the air-raid on Leicester (November 19th 1940) rescue workers (no doubt due to local mining influences) found that tunnelling to rescue trapped casualties was far quicker and safer than the usual painstaking and dangerous method of digging down from the top. This fact was "Picked up" by the Home Office (from Leicester A.R.P. Reports) and as a result, this method of rescue was adopted by all the cities throughout the U.K. and in fact is still in use to this very day, worldwide.

Points to ponder

Whispering Panes.

Probing fingers, caressed the sky
Searchlights, seeking aircraft high
Our shelter abandoned, so cold, so damp
Smelling of moulding blankets, candles, a paraffin lamp.

Moonlight filled my room this night
Blackouts wide, to give more light
I lay in bed, froze to the quick
Trying to coax warmth from an oven baked brick.

Then the distant skyline changed to show
An eerie, expanding, dark red glow
And from my windows came a whispering swell
A fine vibration, which rose and then fell.

The sound increased as time went by
To fit the glow within the sky
Growing stronger with vibrations blending
To a sound continuous, never ending.

Came realisation, later, with shock so deep
That the sounds I heard as I fell asleep
Were my unforgettable introduction
To the sound of carnage, death, destruction.

Coventry , November 14/15th. 1940.

The first vivid wartime memory of the author, as witnessed from Leicester.

Join the men who are hitting HARD!

A typical advert of the day.

Foreword

   I have not found it a pleasant task to comply with the wishes of the Editor by compiling a report on the air attacks in 1940-41, taken from the notes set down in my daily diary at that time. These operational flights over England, right at the beginning, were not the only experiences in which I played a part, but are ones which I would have been glad to have seen included since almost all entries from my diary, when I now read them, give an impression of particular anxiety. This aspect is, however, for the most part completely absent in the usual war reports, which exclude fear and portray only 'heroic deeds'. For today, in a completely peaceful era and nearly fifty years later, the mental environment in which the crew of a bomber plane lived, felt and acted in those times, with the surrounding turmoil of war itensifying daily, cannot be understood by a generation born later.

   What sort of young men were these, who took off day and night at their own risk, carrying heavy bomb loads, and who knew that with their bombs they had hit and destroyed not only ports, docks and industrial targets but cities as well? Were they creatures just full of arrogance and with no feelings?

   Or were they youths who needed all their strength for overcoming their daily fears, in order to give true service to their Fatherland with the humanitarian thoughts of individuals succumbing to the tremendous momentum of the immense efforts of enemies grimly making war on each other?

Robert Götz
Ex Luftwaffe
Airgunner/Observer.

Regensburg, 14. Mai 1986

The above 'Foreword' appears in "The Blitz Then and Now" Vol.1 (After The Battle Publications Ltd.) the editor, Winston G. Ramsey, had asked the writer, Robert Götz (who flew 39 bombing operations over Britain) to supply accounts of his experiences, taken from his daily diaries, in order to enable readers to appreciate what it was like 'for the other side'. They make emotive reading. I include this 'Foreword' for the very same reason. Who knows? Robert Götz could have been involved in any one of the incidents covered by this book!

Who would have thought...?

   In the early days of the war a local civil defence officer received a request from a resident in Long Whatton (Leicestershire) for advice on the best type of Air-Raid Shelter to install. The officer remembers at the time, thinking the most unlikely area to be bombed in the county would be Long Whatton! On the night of 28th August 1940, the first fatal casualty within the county occurred when a young lady, Ellen Burrell, age 20 was killed when a bomb fell on Brook House, The Old Rectory... ...Long Whatton!

   No one, nowhere, was safe in those days.

Why I am proud to be English.

"My word! That was a big chap!"

   I have often heard people ask how we reacted to the bombing during the war. The quote above was taken from a true story in a letter which appeared in the 'Leicester Mercury', in response to requests for stories on the Leicester air raid on the night of 19th November 1940.

   "The quote, sums up the classic response shown many times during the blitz. The story relates to an elderly gentleman who, experiencing his first air raid, and hearing bombs dropping, decided to don his bowler, take his walking stick and go out for a walk to see what was going on. He had not gone far when he met an air-raid warden who told him he should not be out and should be in a shelter. It was at this point a landmine floated above their heads - the warden jumped over a garden wall for cover - but our hero stood his ground and after the explosion, helped the warden back over the wall and with the words "My word! That was a big chap!" then continued, quite unperturbed, on his tour of the 'goings on'."

SOUTH WIGSTON: 1945. Showing Wigston marshalling rail yards centre and South Wigston bottom left.

R.A.F. Photo ©1945

Decoy sites ("Starfish")

After the bombing of Coventry (November 14th 1940) urgent plans were made to construct decoy sites 'Starfish' to attract bombers away from cities. These sites were constructed to form a pattern of fires and lights to resemble burning or poorly blacked out buildings and marshalling yards. 'Starfish' consisted of trenches and structures fitted with lights and petrol/oil burners which were electrically ignited. There were five sites in the county and one or two dummy flare paths, for airfields.

Sites had to be located in an area most likely to be on the flight path of incoming bombers. Timing of ignition had to be perfect and would take place after the first incendiary bombs had been dropped on the target. It was then to be hoped that these could be quickly extinguished and following aircraft would bomb on the decoys. I have no record of the sites around Leicester being fired but some degree of success was obtained by other sites in the UK.

Two other sites in the area were at Gaulby to resemble a certain factory in Leicester (the identity of which I have been unable to establish) and another site at Diseworth, possibly to attract bombs away from the Rolls Royce factory in Derby.

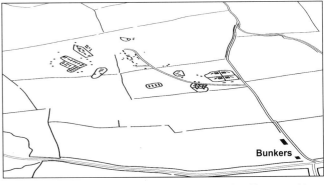

Possible layout for the Starfish site at Beeby. To resemble London Road Railway Station complex.

English Heritage, © Crown copyright

BEEBY: March 4th 1944. This site was intended to resemble the London Road Railway Station and goods yards.

R.A.F. Photo © 1945

NEWTON HARCOURT: February 27th 1945. Constructed to resemble the Railway Junction at Knighton. Situated north of Gorse Spinney, Newton Harcourt.

English Heritage, © Crown copyright

WILLOUGHBY WATERLESS: March 3rd 1944. Constructed to resemble Wigston Railway Junction *(see page 22)*.

Electronic Warfare (X-Beams)

On the night of November 19th 1940 the Luftwaffe used directional radio 'X' beams to attack Birmingham. We cannot be sure if these beams were also used by the pathfinders to attack Leicester but if this was the case, the diagram shows the possible beam settings. The computer signal beam was used by the bomb aimer to activate a crude onboard mechanical computer which calculated the time for bomb release. This could account for the incendiaries in open ground in Wigston and Oadby and the bombs at Stretton Hall and Kirby Muxloe.

Bedlam in Belvior.

During the war the general populations new nothing of radio beams and target maps etc. used by the Luftwaffe to attack our cities. It was commonly thought that the explanation of bombs being dropped in any area was due to the following:

- Aircraft circled around looking for trains to follow.
- Poor or faulty blackouts.
- And (true to tradition) smokers were blamed for lighting up their pipes or 'Park Drive' when bombers were overhead!

It was many years after the war before they became aware that radio beams had been used to guide the bombers to cities and targets.

The first beams to be used were adapted from a system developed as a blind landing aid and was codenamed "Nickobien", this was later improved to a much finer beam and greater accuracy and became known as "X" Verfahren (this beam was used on the first Coventry raid). Further developments gave birth to the "Y" Verfahren which was based on in-built range finding capabilities which proved to be very accurate. However, at the same time our own 'Boffins' were desperately trying to find ways to counter these beams by bending or distorting the signals to confuse the bomber crews to

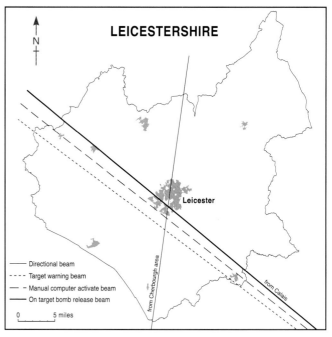

RADIO BEAMS: Possible cross beams over the county.

bomb off target! As our 'Boffins' had to rely heavily on the decoding of the Enigma signals to establish the beam setting this proved to be a difficult task but they did have some success, more so in the later "Y" Verfahren system, where they found it easier to interfere with it's range finding system and cause bombers to overshoot the target. A classic example of this countermeasure, it appears, happened in our own county and was in fact mentioned in Winston Churchill's war memoirs.

On the night of May 8th 1941 Sheffield, Derby and Nottingham were all major targets selected to be attacked. Sheffield was to be the main attack but the first crews to arrive reported very poor visibility and the main force were redirected to bomb Hull.

In the meantime, aircraft which should have been bombing Derby found they were bombing Nottingham. Crews reporting they had bombed Nottingham had, it appeared, bombed the Vale of Belvior! Of the 44 aircraft assigned to Derby only 21 arrived (7 of which had already dropped half their load on Nottingham before they realised they were over the wrong target!) 95 bombers did get through to Nottingham and Beeston but the remainder dropped many tons of bombs in the Vale. Some sources after the war suggested this "mistake" was due to the decoy site at nearby Tithby, but it has since been found that all attempts to ignite this site on the night, failed!

Confusion within the Luftwaffe crews that night was certainly shared by the inhabitants of the villages and hamlets in the Vale of Belvoir who suddenly found hundreds of high explosive, and many thousands of incendiary bombs, falling around their ears! All which fell within one hour. However, apart from slight glass and tile damage to properties, the only casualties were two luckless chickens. On the page opposite are copies of the original A.R.P. reports of the incident, *(see also page 26)* which make fascinating reading!

VALE OF BELVOIR: A.R.P. Civil Defence report map revealing the locations to where H.E. bombs and Incendiaries fell in the district.

GROUP WARDEN'S REPORT ON AIR RAID DAMAGE

GROUP No. 2 (MELTON MOWBRAY DIVISION)

An intense bombing attack developed over the area comprising Bottesford, Normanton, Muston, Easthorpe, Redmile, Barkestone and Plungar on the night of 8/9th. May 1941. The attack commenced shortly after mid-night when bombs were heard in the middle distance. Soon after 00.30 hrs. an arc of exhaust smoke extended from distant south over the villages to distant north.

There quickly followed the light of an incendiary bomb to the S.W. of Bottesford, apparently not far away from the village. All Wardens, Messengers, First Aid and Fire Brigade services on duty were requested to remain doubly alert as developments were intensifying in the surrounding distance.

At approx. 00.45 a blaze of incendiary light was observed in the direction of Barkestone. Contact was immediately made with Barkestone Post Office (acting for Barkestone Wardens). It was reported from there that large nu ber of incendiaries had fallen between Barkestone village and Belvoir Woods. These were promptly dealt with. H.E. bombs then began to fall.

A second fall of incendiaries out at Plungar shortly afterward burst into full light, followed quickly by a similar out-break on the north side of Bottesford near Three Arches Railway Bridge.

From that time on for nearly an hour, H.E. bomb explosions were almost continuous in all quarters of the compass, around Bottesford.

Aircraft were continually over-head. Streaks of exhaust smoke caused patterns in the sky like huge nets. An extensive red glow in the west spread to large proportions. Overhead activity seemed to increase, suggesting that enemy aircraft attempting to get through to the distant fire were meeting opposition.

From that point bombs crashed in all directions.

Frequent contacts were made with Barkestone, Redmile and all Bottesford points. Personal contact with Wardens at Normanton produced report Public Works party had had works under observation as well as the Wardens and that there was no damage to report.

The first damage report came from Bottesford West signal box that near-by railway line had been damaged. Following quickly came the report of bombs and of an un-exp oded bomb in Barkestone village. This was immediately followed by a report that the Bottesford-Harby main road was blocked between Redmile Cross Roads and Barkestone Cross Roads. Preliminary reports to Melton Report Centre were made. Contact with Sergt Beswick was made and an arrangement to meet at Plungar where another un-exploded bomb had been reported, was made. Supt. Stapleton, Sergt. Beswick, Mr Littlejohn (Roa & Bridges) and Mr. Hesford (R.D.C.) met us first at the blocked part on the Bottesford/Harby road. Red lights were affixed by Mr. Littlejohn and steps were taken to man road at diversion points.

At. Barkestone Village several craters and an unexploded bomb crater were inspected. Local house-holders were warned and advised to remain on side of house farthest from bomb.

At Plungar more craters were visited. An unexploded bomb near Council Houses rendered it necessary to advise temporary evacuation to Village Institute. Exploded bomb craters in fields within a few yards of Council Houses caused no damage to life or to house property.

A railway employee reported at Plungar that the Railway Line was damaged near Granby Road bridge, and that steps had been taken to close the line to traffic. Inspection confirmed the damage. Several additional H.E. craters were in the field near railway.

As dawn broke, we were able to see scores of H.E. craters and traces of hundreds of burnt out incendiaries.

At Redmile, bomb craters were also scattered in fields surrounding the village. Several windows in Redmile village including two shops and Methodist Church were damaged.

An unexploded bomb in unfrequented open country at Muston exploded on the morning of 10th May, and one at Plungar during the night.

In spite of this terrific bombardment I am pleased to be able to report that no casualties and no serious damage to property resulted in this Group.

No. 2 GROUP(MELTON DIVISION). PREVIOUS REPORT 10th. MAY.

A final survey of the places damaged during the Air Raid on 8-9 May 1941, shows that the main attack in this County covered an oblong area approx. 7 miles long by 3 miles wide. This included all the villages and hamlets from Normanton (Bottesford)to Plungar). The contiguous county west of this line shows results of equal activity - a point mentioned to show the scale of attack.

Among the articles recovered were several incendiary bomb carrying rods (Fig." in handbook "Objects dropped from the air". These have been deposited at the police station.

The survey reveals an extensive use of incendiary bombs.

In addition to ordinary H.E. bombs, there were about 12 V.I.B. Roads at Barkestone and Plungar have been closed, military guards posted, and notices placed on gates etc.; in addition to evacuation mentioned in my previous report.

Before ending this report I should like to pay a tribute to the work of the Wardens and Messengers in the villages. These kept up constant patrols and observation duties throughout the period of attack. Frequently pieces of shrapnel and the whine of falling bombs caused Wardens to 'hug the road' but nowhere was there the slightest sign of fear or unsteadiness. Having regard to the small establishment and the magnitude of the incident, the situation was splendidly dealt with, and evidences were that that had the damage been more personal to life and property the same coolness would, I am sure, have been shown. As it was the general public seemed greatly heartened by the knowledge that the Wardens were near at hand.

The following is an approx. summary of exploded bombs:-

Place	INCENDIARIES	H.E.
BOTTESFORD and HAMLETS.	Numerous	15
REDMILE	few	46
BARKESTONE	numerous	45
PLUNGAR	numerous	65
	Total	171

Bottesford,
Nottingham.
10th, May 1941

[signature]
Group Warden.

Later counts of craters and U.X.B.'s brought this figure nearer to 250. (This figure does not include bombs which fell over the border into nearby Nottinghamshire.) One U.X.B. which fell in the canal near Redmile could not be removed due to being well below the water table, in silt.

Ammunition Dumps

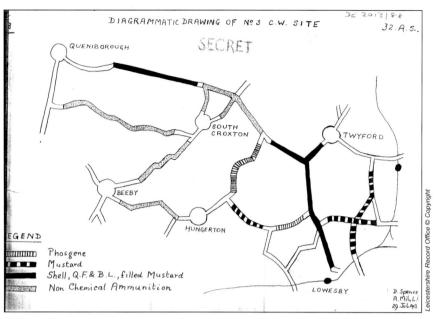

DIAGRAMMATIC DRAWING OF Nº3 C.W. SITE

SECRET

Leicestershire Record Office © Copyright

LEGEND

- ⬛ Phosgene
- ⬛ Mustard
- ⬛ Shell, Q.F. & B.L., filled Mustard
- ⬛ Non Chemical Ammunition

D. Spence
A. Mil. L.
29. Jul. 43

AMMUNITION STORAGE MAP: An official location map for N.E. Leicestershire.

R.A.F. Photo ©1945

AMMUNITION DUMPS: Lining the road between Plungar and Barkestone.

Many ammunition dumps lined the county roads. Above is an example of the maps produced by the council covering Leicestershire. The photo's below show the villages of Plungar and Barkestone-le-Vale during 1945.

The depressions and scars in the landscape could have been the result of the bombing, but only the locals would know. Note the ammunition dumps lining the roads.

R.A.F. Photo ©1945

PLUNGAR: 1945.   **BARKESTONE-LE-VALE:** 1945.

EAST GOSCOTE: 1945. Showing the Royal Ordnance Depot. Melton Road, right.

This photo shows the Royal Ordnance Depot, as it was in 1945. Early in the war it manufactured detonators, fuses and other munitions and was later taken over by the Royal Army Ordnance Corp. Information on its use during this time is very scanty! I do remember seeing many field/anti-tank guns lining the perimeter but whether these were manufactured here or it was a storage depot, cannot be determined. The site was cleared after the war and Jelsons built what is now the East Goscote estate.

BARKBY LANE: 1945. Showing the Anti-Aircraft Battery. The searchlights were on Sandpit Lane, Thurmaston.

Above shows the Anti-Aircraft battery off the Barkby Lane, presumably to protect the Ordnance Depot and other sensitive industries on the Melton Road. I understand from local eye witnesses that this battery fired it's guns on 3 occasions (dates and times unavailable) results are also not to hand apart from a report that when this area and site was machine-gunned by an armed reconnaissance aircraft, a Lewis gunner returned the fire, damaging the plane which eventually crashed in Norfolk. Without dates I have been unable to obtain official confirmation of these incidents. The camp was used as a P.O.W. repatriation camp at the end of the war.

CRASH SITE

R.A.F. Photo ©1945

THURNBY LODGE: This photograph shows the Thurnby Station as it was in 1945.

To the right, taken by sheer chance, can be seen the five craters left as a result of the crash of the Lancaster Bomber on April 8th 1945. From the height taken, the line of craters look insignificant. However, they do stretch for 60 feet and the four engine craters, such was the impact, were at least 10 feet deep. The area is now the built-up Thurnby Lodge Estate and the crash site is across the corner of Thurncourt/Drumcliff Road. A memorial plate on the buttress of the small bridge on Drumcliff Road indicates the spot. This aircraft, from North Luffenham, crashed after the pilot lost control during a fighter affiliation exercise. All six crew members died.

V1 Bomb

R.A.F. Photo ©1945

Glebe Farm, Skeffington

Sitting quietly minding it's own business - far away from wartime activity - was shaken in the early hours of December 18th 1944, when it became host to the only 'V1 flying bomb' to fall in Leicestershire.

This flying bomb, launched from a Hienkel bomber off the east coast, was part of the efforts of the Germans to demoralise the population of the Midlands and the Northern towns in revenge of the destruction of their own cities. Six or seven were launched that night - one also fell in Rutland and the rest in Lincolnshire, Derbyshire and Nottinghamshire.

The flying bomb had the blast destructive power equal to the 1000kg parachute mine (almost double present day SCUD and Tomahawk long range missiles) and would have left a crater in soft earth approx. 30 ft. diameter x 5 ft. deep. The farm suffered light structural damage.

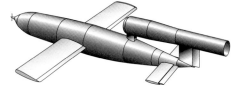

V-1 flying bomb (Doodlebug/Buzz-bomb)

KIRBY MUXLOE: 1945. Castle and moat, top right.

Kirby Muxloe

There is some justice to the wartime claim that Kirby Muxloe was the worst bombed village in England. At 8pm on November 19th 1940 a pair of 500kg parachute mines fell destroying the 'free' church, school rooms and 7 houses. The Post Office and Telephone exchange were severely damaged.

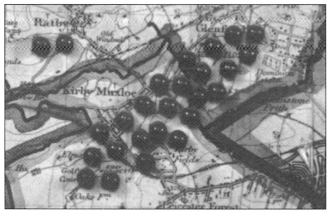

KIRBY MUXLOE: A.R.P. Civil Defence report map.

357 Houses suffered blast damage and over 300 people were made homeless *(see A.R.P. Report, page 20)*.

What is remarkable about this incident is that only 13 people were injured! Sadly, one lady, seriously injured, died later. These low casualty figures could be due to the fact that the Church became the 'Saviour' of the night, as one mine fell within the building which effectually contained most of the blast! The other mine fell close to a house which had solidly built external chimney stacks, which also absorbed most of the blast. However, few people are aware that on that same night, at approximately 10:00pm, two more aircraft dropped another 24 H.E.'s in the area. Thankfully, none hit the village, but one did destroy a water main in the Red Barn area. Whether the activity of rescue teams dealing with the initial bombing attracted the attack, is not known. In addition to the above, it is claimed that yet another Parachute mine (unexploded) was found near to Gullets Lane Bridge on the following day!

The above photo shows the village as it was in 1945. The cleared bomb sites of the church and other buildings are arrowed where the mines fell.

ENDERBY: 1945. Carlton Hayes Hospital bottom centre.

Enderby

This village escaped serious incidents apart from the night of November 1st 1940, when 4 heavy high explosive bombs were dropped in the Enderby Hall area. The Lodge was severely damaged along with gravestones on the nearby cemetery. The two occupants of the Lodge were found buried and injured. One bomb failed to explode and was detonated by a disposal unit the following day. However, Carlton Hayes Hospital and many other properties both in Narborough and Huncote, suffered heavy blast damage when a parachute mine exploded above Tom Webster's farm on the Copt Oak Road.

NARBOROUGH ROAD: Anti-Aircraft & Searchlight battery on the junction of Narborough Road - Leicester Lane.

BRAUNSTONE: Braunstone park and Hockley farm during 1945.

The above photograph is interesting in that it shows many wartime features. **1.** The site of the former U.S. 82nd Airborne Division Headquarters camp on the park (which I erroneously reported in my last book had been demolished but now understand this was taken over by the council to ease the desperate housing shortage). **2.** The formation of prefabs on the Hockley Farm, built by P.O.W.'s. **3.** The searchlight battery on the Western Park. **4.** The missing houses on Webster Road and the patch on Cort Crescent where heavy high explosive bombs fell on May 17th 1941.

HINCKLEY AND SKETCHLEY: 1948.

Hinckley & District

Quite a few bombs dropped in this area, in fact, this prompted the Home Security to ask for lists of any large or sensitive military/industries who were in the area to attract this attention! The reply was, apart from the gas works and railway station in Hinckley and a small number of small factories producing war materials, there were no major target worthy sites. However, the geographical position of Hinckley did put it at the "crossroads" of all the activity centred around Birmingham, Coventry, Nottingham and Derby. As a result, the whole area was at considerable risk from aborting or damaged aircraft looking for and unloading bombs on opportunistic targets.

Reports and details I have found are very scanty and I find that the local A.R.P. were criticised for producing late, inaccurate and unsatisfactory reports on incidents in the area. Having said that, I have found a report on the bombing of Hinckley and Burbage, which I have reproduced showing the casualty rate for the three bombs which fell on Merevale Avenue was very high *(page 33)*. They must have been at least 250kg bombs to cause this amount of damage.

Hinckley and it's district was poorly covered by the R.A.F. photo's during the war years. The above photo was taken in 1948 and I include this to show the area before major developments took place but there appears to be no sign of the damage to Merevale Avenue.

HINCKLEY & DISTRICT: A.R.P. Civil Defence report map, plotting the bomb fall in and around the town.

Hinckley Urban District Council.

CLERK,
A. S. ATKINS,
SOLICITOR.

TELEPHONE Nº 685.

Your ref..............

Our ref. JGST/SMA.

Council Offices,

Hinckley.

17th June, 1941.

Dear Sir,

Hinckley Report Centre

With reference to the air raid damage which
occurred on the night of the 16/17th ultimo in Hinckley and
Burbage, County Control may be interested in the under-
mentioned figures relating to damage to property which I
have extracted from this Authority's return which is
being made to the Ministry. I understand that this return
is not absolutely exhaustive as there are still a few very
minor cases of broken windows etc. to be dealt with but
these will probably not total more than about 20.

		Hinckley	Burbage	Total
A.	Totally destroyed	4	-	4
B.	So badly damaged that demolition is necessary	3	-	3
C.	Seriously damaged but capable of repair;			
(a)	Still usable	19	6	25
(b)	Evacuated or to be evacuated	38	7	45
(c)	Slightly damaged (excluding broken windows)	254	207	461
(d)	Broken windows only	92	83	175
		410	303	713

On the night of May 17th 1941, a total of 40 high explosive bombs fell in the Hinckley area (7 were U.X.B.'s) 3 H.E.'s fell on Merevale Avenue. 8 high explosive bombs and several hundred Incendiaries fell at Burbage, and 8 H.E.'s and Incendiaries fell at Sketchley. The casualties below refer to Merevale Avenue.

SUMMARY OF CASUALTIES.

Hinckley U.D. Dead:	4 Men.	6 Women.	1 Child.
Injured & detained in Hospital:	3 Men.	1 Woman.	0 Children.
Injured: Other cases.	0 Men.	9 Women.	2 Children.

MELTON MOWBRAY: 1945.

R.A.F. Photo ©1945

Melton Mowbray and Asfordby

MELTON MOWBRAY: A.R.P. map.

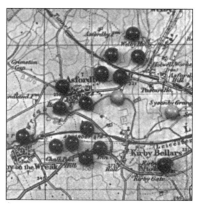

ASFORDBY VALLEY: A.R.P. map.

The town itself suffered only one serious bombing incident when on November 4th 1940 it was attacked at 10.30a.m. by an aircraft which machine-gunned an area from West Avenue to the town centre (bullet scars were reported to be visible on the frontage of the George Hotel for many years.) and dropped four heavy high explosive bombs at Thorpe End, causing one death, three injuries and damage to many houses. On other dates, bombs and incendiaries were also dropped in the Northfield House area near the railway and also an oil bomb at the back of the grammar school. The town was also host to many airborne troops waiting to be dropped in the Arnhem and Rhine crossing operations (via Saltby airfield). Also on the doorstep was the Holwel Iron works, which, being a special target, received special attention from the Luftwaffe and although three or four attempts to bomb this plant failed. (including one daylight attack on October 3rd 1940, when a lone aircraft dropped an 1800kg Satan bomb in a field close to Plants Garage causing a crater approx. 40 ft. diameter x 35 ft. deep.) Sadly, 5 fatalities and 14 injuries occurred when Plants Garage and nearby houses were hit in the Asfordby Valley on the November 23rd 1940. Melton Mowbray was also surrounded by active airfields and quite a number of serious air-crashes were recorded in the close vicinity.

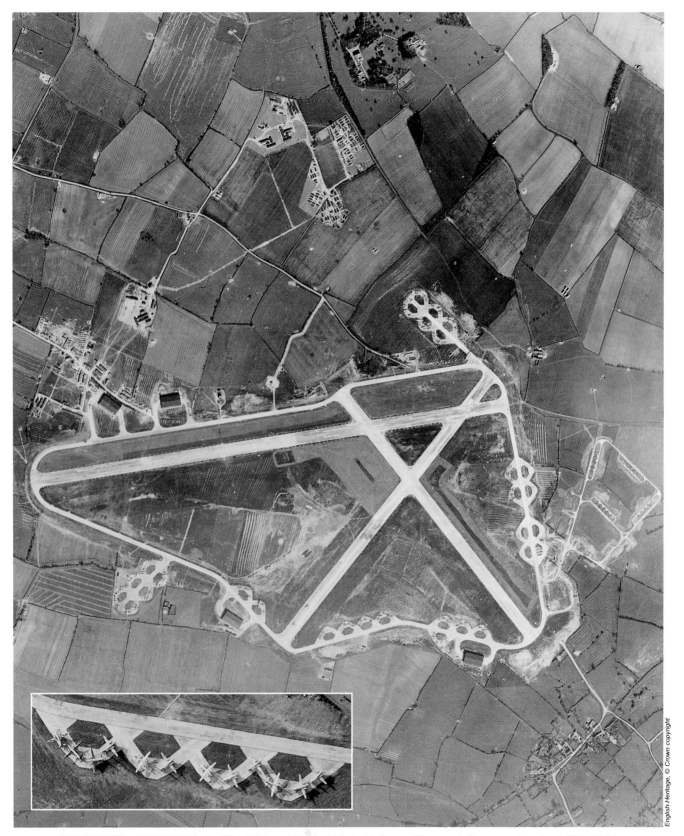

English Heritage, © Crown copyright

RAF MELTON MOWBRAY: No.304 FTU and No.4 OAPU, 44 Group Transport Command on April 18th 1944.
Great Dalby village, bottom right. Inset shows an enlargement of Melton Mowbray Airfield revealing 12 bombers.

Unlike most airfields in Leicestershire, RAF Melton Mowbray appears to have escaped the attention of the Luftwaffe prior to it's opening during August 1943. Melton Mowbray was built to serve as a satellite for RAF Leicester East (Stoughton aerodrome) as an aircraft preparation unit within 44 Group, Transport Command. By October, RAF Melton Mowbray oversaw the formation of No.4 Overseas Aircraft Preparation Unit, along with the arrival of both No.306 and 307 Ferry Training Units (which later merged with 304 FTU). Upon the arrival of No.1 Ferry Crew Pool, in January 1944, RAF Melton Mowbray began preparing a vast array of aircraft for delivery to overseas airfields. As a result, this station housed the likes of: Oxfords, Ansons, Mosquitos, Spitfires, Vengeances, Wellingtons, Beauforts, Hurricanes, Bostons, Liberators, Corsairs, etc. throughout the duration of the war.

MARKET HARBOROUGH: 1945. Great Bowden and Nether Green, top right. Market Harborough bottom left.

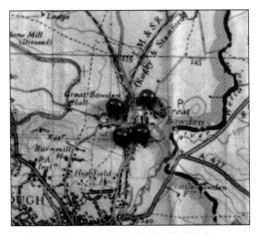

GREAT BOWDEN: A.R.P. Civil Defence report map revealing the locations where H.E. bombs landed in and around the village.

Market Harborough largely escaped the attention of the Luftwaffe during the Second World War. Its nearest raid on record occurred around midnight on the 26th April 1941, at Great Bowden. Records show that there were indeed 4 high explosive bombs which fell on the village. However, rather than falling in a cluster, as shown on the official Civil Defence map *(left)*, the ARP wardens dealing with the incident made clear notes as to them falling in a west to east line across Welham Road and Nether Green, causing 2 slight injuries and blast damage to 87 properties, including the sleeping quarters of some rather bemused evacuees! The likely target for this raid would have been the substantial rail sidings, which are clearly visible above *(top centre)*.

RAF Market Harborough opened during the summer of 1943 for the arrival of No.14 OTU (Operational Training Unit) of 92 Group, RAF Bomber Command. The Wellington bomber (affectionately called 'Wimpies' by aircrews and staff) was the main aircraft to be based at RAF Market Harborough for use by bomber crews in training exercises that involved fighter affiliation (with No.1683 BDTF who move to the station from RAF Bruntingthorpe in February 1944), cross country, night bombing and target practice on local bombing ranges, such as the one used at nearby Mowsley.

RAF MARKET HARBOROUGH: April 22nd 1944. Now the site of Gartree Prison. Foxton village top centre.

LEICESTER EAST AIRFIELD (Stoughton): December 30th 1943. Short Stirling bombers of 3 Group, 196 & 620 Squadrons.

SALTBY AIRFIELD: USAAF Station 538 on March 26th 1944 housing Dakotas with Waco CG-4As and Horsa gliders.

SALTBY AIRFIELD: Luftwaffe photo. November 8th 1940.

Saltby airfield, clearly identified by Luftwaffe reconnaissance aircraft *(left)* 9 months before it was officially opened to house No.14 OTU of 7 Group, in August 1941. This photo would have contributed to the airfield being bombed on at least four occasions during it's period of construction. The first incident was on January 9th 1941 when 3 bombs fell causing damage to a Home Guard hut on Saltby Heath. Further H.E. bombs were dropped coupled with machine gun fire on the airfield during April, followed by two more separate night raids on the 13th and 20th August 1941; ten days before Saltby was officially opened. Note the depressions between runways *(above photo)* which could be the remains of bomb craters.

Saltby airfield is locally famed for its contribution in transporting the 508th Parachute Infantry Regiment, along with a detachment of the 82nd Airborne Division Headquarters unit, to Normandy, June 5th 1944. The 314th Troop Carrier Group of 52nd Troop Carrier Wing, U.S. 9th Air Force Troop Carrier Command later went on to transport men of the 2nd, 3rd, 11th and 156th Battalions of the British 1st Parachute Brigade to Renkum Heath, Arnhem, on September 17th 1944. Elements of the 4th Parachute Brigade were sent to Ginkel Heath the following day, along with the 1st Polish Parachute Brigade on the 19th September 1944.

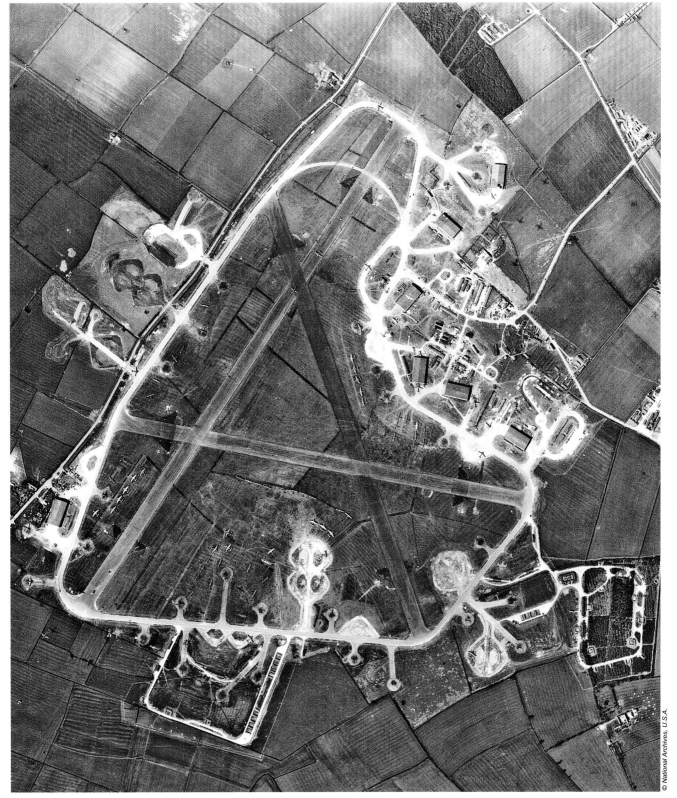

© National Archives, U.S.A.

BOTTESFORD AIRFIELD: USAAF Station 481 on April 18th 1944, the day 440th Troop Carrier Group left for Exeter Airfield.

It didn't take the Luftwaffe reconnaissance long to spot the airfield in early stages of construction. ARP reports reveal the first raid to have occurred was during November 1940, where two high explosive bombs fell between Bottesford and Normanton. RAF Bottesford eventually opened in September 1941 and was to be the only frontline operational airfield in Leicestershire. With the arrival of 207 Squadron a month later, operations began in earnest with the new Avro Manchester, bombing German submarine ports on mainland occupied Europe. By September 1942, 207 Squadron was relocated to RAF Langar, Nottinghamshire, whilst new repair work to the runways were carried out. By November 1942, 90 Squadron of 3 Group was formed, supplied with Short Stirling bombers. The mainly Australian crews of No.467 Squadron (RAAF)

arrived the same month along with their Lancaster bombers. A year later, RAF Bottesford was handed over to the Americans and was subsequently renamed 'Station No.481' of 50th Troop Carrier Wing, 9 Troop Carrier Command. By early 1944, Troop Carrier Groups were carrying out glider towing and paratroop drop exercises with units of the 82nd Airborne Division, which were stationed locally. However, by July 1944, Bottesford returned to RAF control with the arrival of Lancasters and Hurricanes for fighter affiliation training. This activity was to see the final wartime months out for the airfield apart from one final Luftwaffe raid on March 20th 1945. At 10.20pm a lone Ju188 dropped 'Butterfly' bombs on the airfield and machine gunned its hanger, Church Farm, and a train standing at Bottesford railway station - there were no casualties.

© National Archives, U.S.A.

RAF HUSBANDS BOSWORTH: Wellington Bombers of No.14 OTU, 5 Group, Bomber Command on February 29th 1944

RAF Husbands Bosworth began construction in late 1941, but did not open until June 1943. August 1943 saw flights 'A' & 'B' of No.14 OTU, 92 Group, move in with their Wellington bombers from RAF Market Harborough. By June 1944, the station was reclassified into a parent station, and No.14 OTU was renamed No.85 OTU, with no change to operational duties. However, by August 5th 1944 the station saw the arrival of 313th Troop Carrier Group (USAAF) with their C-47 Skytrains used for training preparations for operation 'Market Garden', in Holland. The TCG's stay was short lived and by August 15th they moved on and the station resumed its bomber training duties, as before. No.85 OTU continued to operate until the unit was closed down in June 1945.

RAF Bruntingthorpe housed Wellington bombers of No.29 OTU, 92 Group, Bomber Command. June 1943 saw No.1683 Bomber Defence Training Flight formed and the Tomahawk fighter was used in fighter affiliation exercises with the bombers. No.1683 BDTF moved to Market Harborough in February 1944. By May 1944, No.29 OTU managed to acquire Hurricanes of their own, for use in fighter affiliation exercises.

RAF Nuneaton officially opened in February 1943, but training exercises did not take place until two months after the arrival of No.105 OTU of 44 Group in August 1943. The photograph opposite was taken on the day No.105 OTU was renamed No.1381 TCU of 4 Group for Transport Command.

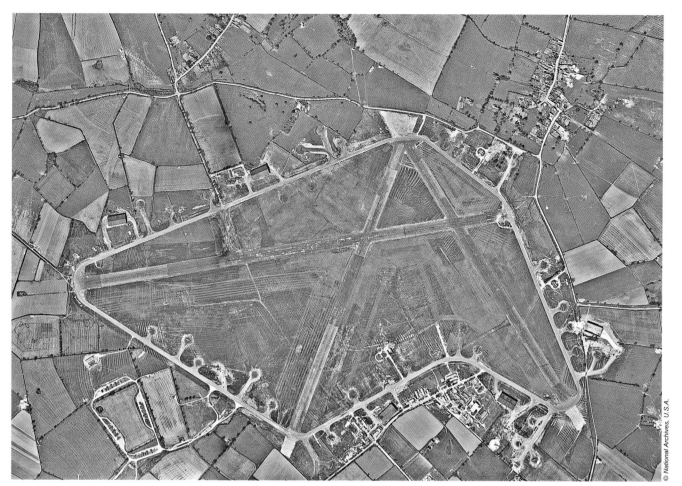

RAF BRUNTINGTHORPE: Wellington Bombers of No.29 OTU, 92 Group, Bomber Command on April 22nd 1944.

RAF NUNEATON (Lindley): Dakotas and Wellingtons of No.1381 Transport Conversion Unit, 4 Group on August 10th 1945.

English Heritage, © Crown copyright

RAF CASTLE DONINGTON: Dakotas of No.108 (Transport)OTU, 44 Group, Transport Command on August 2nd 1945.

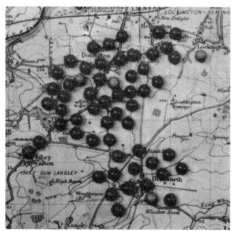

Castle Donington and Diseworth were both bombed in the early hours of August 30th 1940, resulting in minor damage to a few farms and livestock. A second raid occurred in October 1940 followed by a lull in enemy activity, until construction of the new airfield began to emerge. An A.R.P. report clearly states that in the early hours of August 13th 1941, 12 H.E.'s fell 400yds. from the 'new aerodrome' between Gunbro farm and Ashley Road. Almost one year later, Diseworth fell victim to a second raid, no doubt due to it's proximity to the new airfield, when 500 Incendiaries fell on Gelsgoe farm on June 25th 1942.

RAF Castle Donington opened in January 1943, housing units of No.28 OTU from it's parent airfield, at Wymeswold. The Wellington was later replaced with Dakotas by mid October 1944 and No.108 (T)OTU of 44 group, was created to replace No.28 OTU. The above photo was taken 8 days before No.108 (T)OTU was redesignated No.1382 TCU and passed into the hands of 4 Group, Transport Command, whom remained at the airfield until September 1946. Castle Donington survives to this day as East Midlands Airport.

The City 'Stirs'

During my research I came across photographs of the city taken by the R.A.F. during the closing year of the war. I felt I could not leave these unseen in archives and have decided to include these in the book.

These photographs show a city worn out by six years of wartime damage and neglect, no building work had taken place during this time, buses were worn out and continually breaking down, power station generators were on their last legs and there was a severe shortage of all materials. Although some of these photos were taken late afternoon on a Friday rush hour very few cars can be seen and certainly no sign of shopper's due to the fact that most shops had closed by this time and of course they had few goods to sell anyway!

At this time we thought we would soon recover and all would be "rosy" but things were to get worse before they got better! Rationing, lack of fuels, power cuts etc. meant we were ill equipped to deal with the horrendous winter of 1947. I have vivid and painful memories of my family plunging our hands and feet into bowls of snow to relieve the torture of enormous Chilblain's, which resembled bunches of Victoria Plums! The war didn't finish us off, but that winter very nearly did! The following pages will bring back many memories to older readers.

R.A.F. Photo ©1945

LEICESTER UNIVERSITY: Above (facing east) shows the old damaged Pavilion on Victoria Park, bottom right.

I understand that during the 'Hit & Run' period of the Blitz (1942-43) manned anti-aircraft guns were positioned on the sports fields of Wyggeston Girl's School (mid right of photograph) presumably to protect the University (mid left of photograph) which was marked as a primary target. **1.** Air-Raid shelters. **2.** Wyggeston Girls School. **3.** University College.

LONDON ROAD: Shows the cleared bomb damaged sites of the Highfields street and district, middle right.

R.A.F. Photo ©1945

44

HIGHFIELDS: Above shows the cleared bomb damaged sites along Sparkenhoe Street, some with portacabin type buildings erected. Note the circular (now empty) static water tanks on some of the bomb sites. Northampton Square, top right and the old 'Workhouse', mid right below London Road Railway Station.

R.A.F. Photo ©1945

R.A.F. Photo ©1945

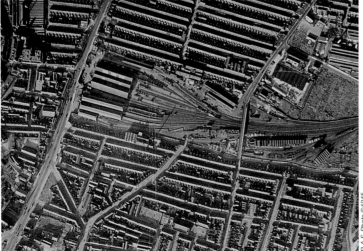

R.A.F. Photo ©1945

▲ **CITY CENTRE:** Above shows the Town Hall and Market top left. Lee Circle and Wharf street centre.

◀ **BELGRAVE ROAD STATION:** This station, soon to become an exodus point for thousands of holiday starved citizens heading for the East Coast resorts, escaped the attention of the Luftwaffe (apart from a few incendiaries) and is now the site of a supermarket.

R.A.F. Photo ©1945

▲ **CITY CENTRE:** Above shows the Castle Gardens, top left and the Great Central Railway Station, top right. The old Lewis' store is bottom right.

BLACKBIRD ROAD STADIUM ▶
Leicester's old speedway/greyhound racing track, off Parker Drive. Now long gone.

R.A.F. Photo ©1945

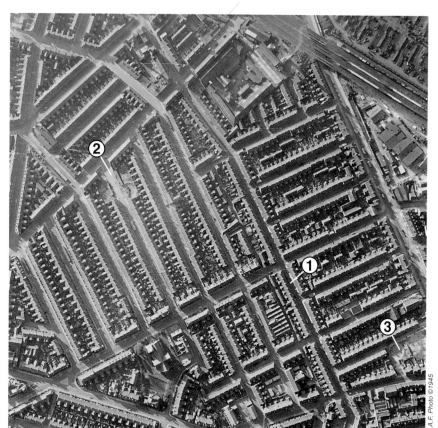

▼ Trocadero

Below can be seen the Leicester Lido **1**, The Trocadero (Cinema and Ballroom) **2** and Humberstone Park **3**, which represented the trio of my main sources of entertainment during the war. With no suntan lotions available, the Lido, having no heating, was visited at the risk of severe sunburn, pneumonia, or both. On the roof of the Trocadero can be seen (end nearest Lido). The air raid siren which was responsible for many a "colly wobble" within the local population.

Humberstone Park was ruled by park keepers with a rod of iron. Singing, music, ballgames, walking on cricket pitches or any other activity was forbidden on Sundays and I will always remember one Sunday when a company of 'Home Guard' descended on the park. The sight of these men in army boots and fixed bayonets practicing section and platoon attacks across the pitches was a sight to behold, and must have shortened the park keepers life considerably!

R.A.F. Photo ©1945

▲ Charnwood Street

Above is the area of the old 'Charny' **1**. which was a very popular shopping area (similar to Pettycoat Lane), which has long since been demolished. Also can be seen are the cleared sites of the two parachute mine incidents which occured on the night of November 19th 1940: Grove Road **2**. and Frank Street **3**. both of which caused trauma to my wife, her family and my own close family *(See dedication in my 1st book 'Birds Eye Wartime Leicester.')* Uppingham Road Right.

R.A.F. Photo ©1945

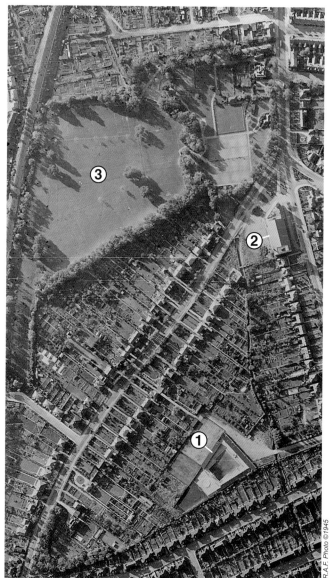

R.A.F. Photo ©1945

▲ Kenwood Lido

Above is the old Kenwood Lido off Kenwood Road, Knighton. Carisbrooke Road, (right).

HUMBERSTONE VILLAGE: August 1945. Manor Farm, top centre. Note the remains of the 'C' shaped Medieval fish pond or 'Moat' behind Arncliffe Road, middle left, which has long since gone.

R.A.F. Photo ©1945

49

SCRAPTOFT: 1945. Repatriation camp on former site of the U.S. 82nd Airborne Division's 'Camp March Hare' 325th G.I.R.

THURNBY: 1945. Coles nurseries, top left.

STOUGHTON: 1945. Searchlight and Anti-Aircraft Battery, top right.

BUSHBY: 1945.

EVINGTON: 1945. Shady Lane Repatriation camp on the site previously occupied by the U.S. 82nd Airborne Division's 504th Parachute Infantry Regiment. Note the worn patches made by the previous tented areas of the camped regiment.

CITY GENERAL HOSPITAL: 1945. A busy hospital, but note the absence of motor cars. No parking problem here! The old cindered rutted 'Cut-throat Lane' (now Coleman Road) can be seen on the right, together with the entrance to the 'Waterworks', top right.

WIGSTON MAGNA: 1945.

Rowlatts Hill

AMBASSADOR ROAD: Off Wicklow Drive.
The formation of Prefabs in 1945.

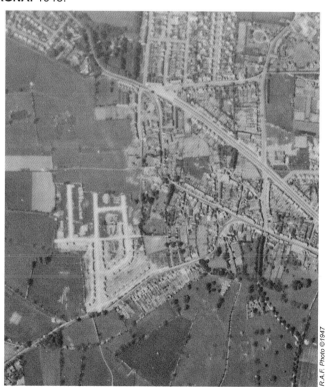

BRABAZON ROAD: Oadby in 1947.
The birth of Brabazon Road Estate.

P.O.W.'s were involved in the construction of both these sites after the war.

R.A.F. Photo ©1945

BLABY: 1945.

Bibliography

Bonser, R. 2001 "Aviation in Leicestershire and Rutland" Midland Counties Publications, Leicestershire, England.

Carswell, J.; Johnson, R. & Kirrane, S. (eds) 1989 "Ours To Defend... Leicestershire's people remember the home front." The Leicester Oral History Archive & The Mantle Oral History Project.

Cartwright, T.C. 1998 "Birds Eye Wartime Leicester" TCC Publications, Leicester.

Chorley, W.R. 1992-8 "Royal Air Force Bomber Command Losses of the Second World war Vol 1-6" Midland Counties Publications, Leicestershire, England.

Dobinson, C. 2000 "Fields of Deception: Britain's Bombing Decoys of World War II" Methuen Publishing Ltd., London, England.

Halpenny, B.B. 1981 "Action Stations 2: Military airfields of Lincolnshire and the East Midlands" Patrick Stephens Limited, Northants, England.

Holyoak, V. 1995 "On the Wings of the Morning: RAF Bottesford 1941-1945" The Author, Leicester, England.

Home Office 1940 "Civil Defence Office of the Regional Commissioner: North Midland Regional Office, Nottingham." Home Office Security Intelligence Summary. Public Records Office, Kew, London.

Harriman, K. 2001 "Shadows of the Past: Leicester East Airfield (Stoughton)" The Author, Leicester, England.

Leicester Mercury 1946 "Leicester Blitz Souvenir" Adams Bros.& Shardlow / Wright Process Engraving Co. Ltd., Leicester, England.

Masters, C.J. 1995 "Glidermen of Neptune: The American D-Day Glider Attack" Southern Illinois University Press, U.S.A.

McDougall, J. 1979 "Civil Defence In Leicestershire 1935-1945" The Author, Leicester, England.

Moore, L. C. 1996 "Z17 - My War Memories 1939-1945" The Author, Ingatestone, Essex, England.

Nicholls, J. 2000 "England Needs You: The Story of Beaumanor Hall" The Author, Leicestershire, England.

Ramsey, W.G. 1987-89 "The Blitz Then And Now, Vol.1-3" Battle of Britain Prints International Ltd., England.

Smith, D.J. 1989 "Britain's Military Airfields 1939-45" Patrick Stephens Limited, Northants, England.

The Living History Unit. 1996 "Leicester at War November 19th 1996: A guided tour of the sites associated with the Second World War" The Living History Unit, Leicester.

Wilkes, G. 1997 "East Midlands Airport in Wartime" Pentland Press Ltd., Co. Durham, England.

Wills, D. 1992 "Put On Your Boots & Parachutes" The Author, Leicester, England.

Down to Earth

K.W. Palmer ©1940

November 19th 1940

© Wright Process Engravings Co. Ltd.

November 20th 1940

THE LODGE: Elmfield Avenue, Stoneygate.
Home of the Palmer family who miraculously escaped death when the house received a direct hit, but four of the family were injured. Another of the many red spots on the city map.